Manuel Monade moved to the UK in 1987 from Paris where he was studying archaeology and art history at La Sorbonne. In London, he opted for a more hands-on vocational path, first becoming a qualified chef then moving on to baking in various West End restaurants in the exciting London food scene of the 1980s and 1990s. His defining moment came when he joined the original team at St John Restaurant in Smithfield. Fergus Henderson, the head chef and proprietor, insisted on having real artisan bread freshly baked in-house for each service. Dan Lepard was the main baker and he introduced Manuel to breadmaking. When Dan left, Manuel took over the small bakery and never returned to working as a chef again. He baked not only for the restaurant but also for the local community in Farringdon and Clerkenwell. Manuel returned to France to train at the Institut National de la Boulangerie Pâtisserie in Rouen before returning to work in London. For many years he worked with Matt Jones at Flour Power City Bakery, before becoming a teacher at Bread Ahead Baking School. Manuel is the current chair of the Southwark Refugee and Migrant Project, an organisation that he has been working with for the past 20 years. Having helped people facing stressful situations in the course of his charitable work, and also having experienced the sense of achievement of his students, he is interested in the therapeutic potential of baking to enhance wellbeing.

Caroline Harrison is a BABCP-accredited Cognitive Behavioural Therapist and supervisor, EMDR (eye-movement desensitisation and reprocessing) therapist and mental health nurse with over 20 years' experience in the NHS, working in a range of adult, child and adolescent therapeutic services. She currently works at the Centre for Anxiety Disorders and Trauma at the Maudsley Hospital. Caroline authored a workbook on Coping with Trauma in collaboration with the Good Thinking website https://www.good-thinking.uk with techniques for helping people cope with symptoms of PTSD.

Breaditation
DE-STRESS BY MAKING BREAD

MANUEL MONADE
WITH CAROLINE HARRISON

ROBINSON

ROBINSON

First published in Great Britain in 2021
by Robinson

10 9 8 7 6 5 4 3 2

Copyright © Manuel Monade, 2021

Bread Making for Mental Wellbeing
Copyright © Caroline Harrison, 2021

The moral rights of the authors have been
asserted.

A CIP catalogue record for this book is
available from the British Library.

ISBN: 978-1-47214-684-7

Typeset in Great Britain by
Mousemat Design Limited

Printed and bound in Great Britain by Clays
Ltd, Elcograf S.p.A.

Papers used by Robinson are from well-
managed forests and other responsible
sources.

MIX
Paper from
responsible sources
FSC® C104740

Robinson
An imprint of
Little, Brown Book Group
Carmelite House
50 Victoria Embankment
London EC4Y 0DZ

An Hachette UK Company
www.hachette.co.uk

www.littlebrown.co.uk

The recommendations given in this book are
solely intended as education and should not be
taken as medical advice.

This book is dedicated to anyone who is struggling to cope with daily life, who is feeling isolated or perhaps even lacking self-worth. We humbly hope that using your hands to make bread and to bake — this simple way of being proactive — may play a small role in your recovery.

Contents

Preface

Before there was a book, there was a project.

I have been working with refugees and asylum seekers in the London Borough of Southwark for over 20 years as the chair of the Southwark Refugee and Migrant Project. I had been interested for a while in linking my professional baking experience directly to my voluntary work through some meaningful initiative. I thought first about a bakery as a social enterprise to tackle the high rates of unemployment in refugee communities, but I wasn't sure that I could commit to such an initiative in the long term, or if I would be able to devote the energy needed to make it successful. I carried on with my day job, but this idea was always at the back of my mind, popping up from time to time, although more as a bitter-sweet thought: 'It could have been a great idea.'

Then, entirely by chance, I met Caroline Harrison through a common acquaintance in the voluntary sector. We started to talk about our respective lines of work. She told me that she was a cognitive behavioural psychotherapist at the South London and Maudsley NHS Foundation Trust specialising in trauma and anxiety disorders, and part of her job (aside from individual therapy) was to run groups for people who had been through distressing or traumatic experiences in the past. To me, this presented an unexpected opportunity to unearth my old idea. I would just have to change it from a straightforward employment venture to more of a general wellbeing project. Naturally, I asked Caroline if she would be interested in adding baking as another activity to her weekly therapy group. She thought that this sounded like a great idea, but she would have to discuss it with the rest of her team. In the opinion of an impatient baker that took quite some time! But eventually things started to happen quickly and we were soon ready to launch our long-awaited project. Twenty-twenty seemed a promising year, but then, as we all know, the whole world ground to a halt, and it was impossible in the short term for workshops to go ahead. Once again, 'It could have been a great idea'!

But in another twist of fate, through another chance encounter, this time with publisher Duncan Proudfoot who happened to be attending one of my breadmaking classes, the idea bounced back and became the potential subject for a book, this time aimed at a much wider audience, but with the same ultimate goal: to look at baking as a way to unwind and ground ourselves, to help us cope with stress. In many ways, the craze for baking during the first lockdown had already made that case.

Through its various reincarnations, this idea remained essentially the same: to use baking as a medium for positive personal change. And I'm still hopeful that those workshops that had to be postponed will come to fruition in the not too distant future, turning that slow-proving idea into practice.

Manuel Monade

Introduction

Breaditation: The Art of Bread Making

Breaditation is the act of gathering four simple ingredients – flour, water, yeast and salt – then combining them, kneading them into a dough, leaving the dough to prove, shaping it, baking it and taking it out of the oven. Now we can rename it my bread, smell it and break it with our hands, eat it and feel utterly good about oneself. Although that is not a very academic definition, it is an emotional one that captures the essence of breadmaking for me. We might begin with a pun, but *Breaditation* has at its heart the aim of helping people in practical ways to find peace.

Having been a professional baker for so many years, and having recently begun to teach the general public how to make bread at Bread Ahead Bakery School, something that has always struck me about breadmaking is the emotional impact of seeing a loaf, made with one's own hands, coming out of the oven. And it doesn't matter if you are a seasoned professional baker or a domestic baker. You will be under that same spell each time your bread emerges beautifully from the oven. Mastering the whole process of creating a loaf of bread will always generate a strong feeling of pride and a sense of absolute achievement. To instil those powerfully positive emotions is the aim of this book, the true motivation behind it.

Working through the process of breadmaking

I suspect that most people skip the introduction in a cookery book, impatient to get straight to the recipes, but please bear with me in this case and spend a little more time reading these preliminary instructions, as they will be providing some valuable information to send you on your merry baking way.

This book is suitable for complete beginners, but also for more advanced home bakers who haven't made bread for some time and who might need to brush up on their baking knowledge. It's for people who might have embarked on learning how to bake during the first lockdown and feel drawn to continue, and for anyone looking for a relaxing hobby – a peaceful haven of 'me time' – but who have little or no baking experience. If you have no grounding in the basics of baking, you might be wandering in the wilderness for a long time, making the same mistakes on the way. Mistakes are fine if you learn from them and then progress, but if you are repeating the same mistakes again and again, you have a problem! If that is happening to you, you will not be progressing, and a string of failures just leads to frustration, probably leading you to throw in the towel. Frustration is not relaxing, as we all know.

In the following pages you will find a lot of emphasis describing in detail the different stages involved in breadmaking. It is important to deconstruct the baking process into stages and to outline precisely the essential information within those stages, then to repeat that information almost on loop mode to help you remember it until it becomes second nature. I apologise in advance for what might seem to be lengthy, or even hypnotically repetitive, descriptions. It is for your own good, however. Repetition is the basis of solid learning.

I have also opted for a limited number of recipes so that readers will not be overwhelmed with a long list of recipes that most of us will almost certainly not have time to make. My intention was to reduce the list to a reasonable number of basic recipes using different ingredients, skills and equipment so that everyone can have a go at all of them in a relatively short space of time. That, I hope, will give you a sense of achievement, and that will boost your confidence and keep you motivated to carry on for, hopefully, a very long time. This book's main ambition is to initiate a personal journey into breadmaking as a way of contributing to healthy eating, but perhaps even more importantly, general wellbeing through the productive use of our hands, our senses and the stimulation of our mind.

Basic baking recipes

You might feel like a relaxing break from all that kneading, so I have also included three basic pastry recipes for you to perfect, giving you the opportunity to make a number of pastry-based dishes, such as pies, tarts and confectionery, once you have mastered those techniques. I also include a useful and simple biscuit and a cracker recipe to add to your repertoire.

Bread Making for Mental Wellbeing, by Caroline Harrison

Imagine you are in your kitchen, perhaps listening to something good on the radio. You've weighed out some strong white flour into a bowl, added the precise amount of yeast, salt and some cool or warm water, depending on the temperature outside. You start to mix the ingredients with one hand, catching them all up into a malleable ball of dough. You tip it out of the bowl onto a surface and begin to work it. You can smell the yeast and feel the stickiness on your palms and fingers as you knead and work the dough. You're completely absorbed in what you're doing, and what you can see, observing how the dough is changing and deciding whether it is ready to rest, prove or if it needs more kneading. You take your scraper and pull it all back together, then continue. You might feel the warmth from the oven as you preheat it, your arms might feel tired if it's a dough that requires a lot of kneading, but your body feels relaxed. You can see your dough expanding as it proves. You might have something already baking in the oven and be able to smell that, triggering happy nostalgia. The repetitive action of kneading, working and slapping the dough allows your mind to idle in neutral, just observing the action, not worrying about any of life's stresses, completely absorbed and focused only in the moment.

Had you told me a few years ago that I would be writing a chapter in a breadmaking book I would have looked at you in disbelief. I'd never baked bread before and my previous attempts at baking anything had been mostly disastrous. When I met Manuel, this changed.

Manuel and I have both worked extensively with refugees; Manuel as chair of the Southwark Refugee and Migrant Project and me in my role as a cognitive behavioural and EMDR therapist treating post-traumatic stress disorder (PTSD), anxiety disorders and depression.

When we met, he told me of his desire to set up a therapeutic baking group for survivors of trauma, which he wanted to call Breaditation, as he felt that the process of breadmaking was mindful, meditative and grounding. We had an interesting discussion about the benefits of this, and when he needed a trauma therapist to co-facilitate the group, I leapt at the opportunity. I explained that I had no breadmaking skills, nor any great love of baking at that point, but he assured me that he could change that.

Over the next few months, we met up to arrange the Breaditation group, initially for refugees, which was a collaboration between the Centre for Anxiety Disorders and Trauma (the NHS clinic where I work) and Bread Ahead, Manuel's baking school. It was to run from Mental Health Week in May to Refugee Week in June 2020. Unfortunately, the lockdowns as a result of the COVID-19 pandemic derailed this plan, but the concept of Breaditation seemed more apt and necessary than ever, so the idea for this book was conceived. Along the way I have had the privilege to be taught some of the recipes in this book by Manuel over video calls and to reap some of the therapeutic benefits myself, which go much further than my obvious relief at not burning down my kitchen!

This is not a therapy book; it is a breadmaking book. But it exudes wellbeing, filled with all the benefits that breadmaking can bring. The recipes are the real stars here, but in making them you stand to find peace of mind and a sense of achievement.

The following paragraphs are not meant to make false claims about breadmaking as a cure-all, nor are they a self-help guide for coping with different mental health issues, but I have linked some of my knowledge and experience of treating mental health issues to aspects of breadmaking, which some people might find therapeutic.

What are some of the therapeutic effects of breadmaking?

When I work with clients suffering with PTSD, anxiety, depression or any other mental health difficulty, one of the first things we assess alongside their symptoms is how much the problem is impacting on their day-to-day life. Is there anything they have stopped doing? Is the problem making them avoid things they used to enjoy? Typically, a goal of treatment is getting the client to recover activities that they used to enjoy doing before the mental health problem interfered, and to reclaim their lives. Most mental health services have occupational therapists (OTs) working as part of their multi-disciplinary teams, because the value of engaging people in therapeutic activity is well known. I have worked with some great OTs (and other mental health professionals) who see baking and breadmaking as therapeutic. Below are some of the reasons this could be.

Breadmaking is grounding

When I work with clients who have PTSD, they frequently re-experience a past traumatic event through flashbacks, nightmares and vivid memories, as if the trauma is happening again in the here and now. This can be very frightening and disorienting, and sufferers understandably start to avoid anything that might trigger this response. They might also feel constantly on the lookout for danger, be jumpy, have strong emotions or feel numb or spaced out.

In the early stages of treatment, I often use grounding techniques to help the client manage these symptoms so that they can feel safer. Grounding involves using your five senses (sight, smell, taste, touch and hearing) to help you notice your current environment and to stay focused on the here and now. They can remind a person with PTSD that the trauma is not happening now, that they survived the traumatic event and are now safe.

Grounding is not just helpful for people with trauma, it can also help anyone who is feeling anxious, angry, upset, a bit spaced out or apart from themselves.

Breadmaking involves all our senses, so it is an excellent grounding activity. The feel of the dough between your fingers and on your hands, kneading and moving it around can really focus you on the present. It can be quite physical at times if it needs to be kneaded quickly, or if the dough is hard. You must look at what you are doing, making sure that the dough is changing (or not) the way you want it to. The smells involved in breadmaking, of yeast, and of dough baking are very evocative, and for some it is very comforting, taking them back to happy memories, perhaps baking with loved ones as a child. At the end you are rewarded with the taste, smell and texture of freshly made bread.

In EMDR therapy, one of the techniques we use with people who are traumatised is to get them to imagine a peaceful place. This is somewhere they can depict themselves where they feel safe and calm, with lots of sensory information about what they can see, hear, taste and smell, also what they can feel in their body, in terms of physical sensations (the sun on my skin, relaxed muscles) and emotions (calm, safe). The idea is to get them to tune in to this peaceful place as often as possible, to give the brain another option rather than always going immediately to the threatening place. Because of its sensory richness, people frequently use baking as an example of a peaceful place. The start of this chapter illustrates this.

When Manuel and I were planning the Breaditation group, we thought that not only would the measuring, kneading and working the dough be grounding, but that the time taken while waiting for the dough to prove could also be therapeutic, as it presented an opportunity for group members to talk and share experiences and techniques that had helped them to overcome their difficulties.

Breadmaking is also reassuringly comforting; no matter how difficult things are, or how long it takes, you can follow a set of instructions and get a tangible reward at the end of it.

Breadmaking can elevate your mood

When people are depressed, they typically feel low in mood, unmotivated and foggy, and they don't have the energy to do much. They might start to feel hopeless or worthless, and their thinking tends to follow their feelings, so they might start to have negative thoughts such as 'I'm useless', 'No one cares', and so on.

When feeling like this it can seem difficult to do everyday activities or see other people, and it's tempting to do nothing and isolate yourself. Unfortunately, if we just stay in bed or do nothing all day it reinforces our negative beliefs about ourselves ('I'm useless, no one cares, I can't even do the simplest thing'), and it drives our mood even lower. But if we engage in activity, despite how we feel, we can start to improve our mood in the long run and reinforce positive beliefs that we can cope ('I felt awful, but at least I got up and had a shower').

When working with depression, one of the early steps in treatment is to help the person plan and engage in activities that give them a sense of achievement, pleasure and connectedness to others, as these types of activities improve people's mood. Breadmaking is an achievement (especially for me) and is also enjoyable. You can make bread with others so it can be social. It's altruistic – something you have done that can bring pleasure to people. The sense of accomplishment can improve self-esteem and self-confidence. Breadmaking is a perfect activity for combating a low mood.

Breadmaking uses skills that can help combat anxiety

When I work with clients with anxiety disorders, they are often preoccupied with what they are thinking and feeling, and can treat their thoughts and feelings as factual evidence that things really are as dangerous and bad as they fear. One of the techniques to counteract this is to shift the focus of attention from inside yourself – for example, 'Are my thoughts normal? Should my breathing be doing that? Am I coming across as boring?' – to an external focus of attention. Breadmaking is an activity that requires your focus of attention to be completely external.

When people are anxious, they frequently focus on the future and what (usually negative) events might happen, even if they are things that they can do nothing about. Imagining and rehearsing feared situations that might never happen, or that you can do nothing about if they do, can be very unhelpful, so we try to get clients to focus instead on concerns that are happening in the here and now that they can do something about. Breadmaking is something you can focus on in the present that you have control over.

When working with clients with obsessive compulsive disorder (OCD), they sometimes report needing to achieve a 'just right feeling'. The continual quest for this can make people believe that they cannot tolerate things not feeling right. One of the plans we had with the Breaditation group was to eventually offer it to clients with OCD, as the kitchen can often be an area of concern for people with contamination fears, and treatment for OCD involves exposing people to feared situations and finding out whether anything bad actually happens and how the world really works. When Manuel was teaching me to bake focaccia and ciabatta, I found the stickiness of the dough adhering to my fingers and the feel of it drying on my hands produced an urge to wash it off, and I thought this could be a good opportunity to help people realise that they can tolerate uncomfortable feelings. Manuel taught me a brilliant technique of rubbing your hands together with flour over the bin to make it easier to use your hands without washing them. But if this feels difficult for you, there are some recipes in this book that produce less sticky doughs, so you might want to work your way up from those to increase your tolerance.

When Manuel was teaching me to bake bread, we made brioche, which required me to work some butter into the dough. I started to overwork it, which made the dough a greasy mess, difficult to work with, and it started to fall apart. I likened this to overthinking, something we all do sometimes when we are anxious. We think it helps, but in reality it's unproductive, takes up too much time and can leave us in a bigger mess than we were before.

Breadmaking as mindfulness

In recent years there has been a lot of research into the benefits of mindfulness: from reducing anxiety and helping people manage their emotions to reducing stress and managing pain. Mindfulness involves purposefully paying attention to the present moment: our thoughts, feelings, sensations and experiences, and it's important to do this without judgement. In practice it means not focussing on the future and what might happen, or on what has happened before in the past, but on what is happening right now. It is being aware of our current situation and observing how we are, in the moment, without criticism. It is not about judging or labelling our reactions, feelings or circumstances as good or bad, and so it cultivates a sense of self-compassion. Being mindful in this way can make us enjoy things more and understand ourselves better.

Breadmaking can be a mindful activity. It can be meditative, and the repetition of the movement can produce a sense of calm and help you focus purely on the here and now. It gives the opportunity to take time out from anxious thoughts and perhaps even allow the subconscious to solve problems as you focus on something else. The fact that it takes time is a reminder to slow down, something we can all do with occasionally.

Breadmaking as an opportunity to practice self compassion

If, like me, you are new to breadmaking, you will probably make a few mistakes along the way.

Self-compassion is important because the way we think about and speak to ourselves has a huge impact on our mental health. Clients I work with always joke that I bang on and on about being kind to ourselves, but if you take the time to notice how you speak to yourself, most of us are pretty self-critical. We wouldn't dream of speaking to others the way we speak to ourselves (I'm so lazy/such a failure for not going to the gym), because they would rightly be hurt and offended. In the same way, self-criticism is extremely detrimental to our mental health. If your loved one said that they didn't go to the gym, you wouldn't attack them, but rather you might say, 'Well you're tired. Have a well-deserved rest; you can always go tomorrow.' We can speak to ourselves in the same compassionate manner and, simply by being kinder to ourselves, can feel comforted, happier and boost our self-esteem. Compassion-focussed therapy helps clients to develop these skills, and it's something that can benefit us all. I told Manuel when we met that I was 'useless' at baking and it would be 'hopeless' to teach me, which was rather self-critical, but breadmaking gave me the opportunity to practise my self-compassion (especially with the English muffins and brioche, where I made a lot of mistakes!).

Breadmaking to de-stress

Making bread is great for de-stressing for all the reasons mentioned above, and I discovered that it's also good when you're feeling irritable and angry. There is nothing better than taking all your frustrations out on a dough that needs a lot of work, repeatedly slapping it down hard on the work surface, when someone has annoyed you.

Breaditation

There is something very special about taking a few ingredients, taking time with them and allowing them to transform into something else. Taking the time to do something for yourself, to create something good to eat and to allow your focus to rest on only what you are doing is nurturing. Crafting something from nothing and expressing creativity is good for our mental health. Grounding ourselves in the here and now, and being mindful is therapeutic. The repetitive action and focus on what we are doing is meditative and can give our stressed-out brains a break. You can vent your frustrations on dough and still have something good at the end of it. Breadmaking takes time and isn't something you have to master in a minute – it can remind us to slow down. Every bake can be different, an accomplishment, and you can learn something new each time. No matter what is going on in your life, if you follow the recipes in this book, you will have a tangible reward at the end of it. And if something does go wrong, as it sometimes will, even for the best bakers, you can simply try again. Breadmaking is a chance to be kind to ourselves, to allow ourselves to make mistakes and to learn from them without judging ourselves, in other words, to practise self-compassion.

This is the concept of Breaditation.

Bread Basics

The Four Stages of Breadmaking

Baking bread is a succession of apparently simple, almost innocuous, actions, but each one of them is a crucial building block en route to producing a great loaf of bread. If your kneading is not properly done, if your proving times have not been correctly observed, if your shaping is not sufficiently tight (for a dough that needs more structuring) and, finally, if you are baking at the wrong temperature, or you have skipped using steam – any one of those stages will have a negative impact on your final loaf of bread.

Kneading

We begin with the first action: kneading. This is the process of bringing together the four basic ingredients in any breadmaking: flour, water, yeast (fresh, dried yeast or a sourdough starter) and salt. You are imposing cohesion and order from a messy beginning. Through kneading, you are going to gradually develop the gluten in the flour into a tight but still elastic matrix, which will trap carbon dioxide (CO_2), one of the by-products of fermentation (alongside alcohol production). The steam created during baking – because as your bread bakes, it boils – will also be partly retained by the developed gluten and will contribute to its final volume.

Creating structure

You don't have to knead the dough for a very long time – I would recommend anything from 6 to 8 minutes, although I will accept 10 on a bad day! Kneading for longer is not going to make the bread taste better. You're not in the realm of the sliced white loaf, to which high-speed mixers give more volume, the reasoning being that if a loaf is big it must be nice: it's not necessarily the case. Kneading for too long can lead to over-developing your dough to the point that the gluten could snap, making the dough completely unusable: very stretchy, a bit like over-chewed chewing gum, but with no strength. It might even begin to leach out some of its water. In a way, you would have deconstructed your loaf before you'd even made it. At that point, you wouldn't have a loaf any more – very sadly, your dough would be ready for the bin. Kneading your dough for too long also oxidises it, making it lose the natural pigmentation of the white flour, which is not, in fact, white, but almost yellow or creamy.

If you are kneading by hand, it would take you a couple of hours to over-develop your gluten, so it's fair to say that it's very unlikely that you would have the physical stamina to keep kneading for that length of time. Using a mixer on high speed, however, for 30 minutes could easily take you into the kneading danger zone. With kneading, then, always remember that less is more.

No-knead baking

Some bakers even champion the no-knead approach, advocating simply bringing the basic ingredients together and leaving the kneading to Mother Nature. The no-knead method is based on the fact that, as soon as the gluten molecules come into contact with the water, they bind together to form that gluten matrix I mentioned earlier. Kneading either mechanically or by hand is simply speeding up that process. A no-knead dough will always be a bit weaker structurally than a fully kneaded dough, and that is why you have to compensate for the lack of structure given by kneading by folding the dough a few times. Folding strengthens the dough and at the same time incorporates more air to regenerate the fermentation. There isn't a no-knead recipe in this book, but you might come across one during your breadmaking journey, so you'll at least have had a glimpse of the principles behind it. Do bear in mind, however, that it is this natural formation of the gluten matrix that is helping you when you knead. It doesn't have to be an extended, strenuous effort.

Be organised before you start

Before you start kneading, make sure that you've got all your ingredients and equipment at hand; the last thing you want is to have to start looking for your salt when your hands are already dripping with dough. Being organised, I find, contributes to a kind of inner peace that will make the whole experience much more gratifying, and will make you much more likely to carry on with baking.

THE ALL-IN-ONE METHOD

I use an all-in-one method of baking when making bread: adding ingredients to my mixing bowl on the kitchen scales and turning the scale to 0g between each added ingredient. I always begin by weighing my yeast. Then, after setting my scale back to 0g, I add my water, then my flour, before finishing with the salt. (Don't forget to set your scale back to 0g between ingredients. Don't try to add them without doing so unless you're very good at mental arithmetic!) It's always important to separate the salt and the yeast. In direct contact with each other the salt might kill the yeast, or certainly it will greatly reduce its effectiveness.

(See page 53 for details about the equipment that you will need to get started with breadmaking.)

Combining the ingredients

Once you've weighed and combined your ingredients, the kneading can begin. Using one hand only, combine the flour, yeast, water and salt together until it forms a dough. It doesn't matter if it is a loose dough at this stage, but you want to make sure that you haven't got any dry flour that is not mixed in lurking in your bowl. It's also very important to regularly scrape the side of the bowl to make sure that all the bits we usually leave behind without thinking are included in the main body of dough that will form our loaf of bread.

Put the contents of your bowl on a work surface without any flour on it. Don't worry if it looks like a sloppy mess at this stage. Why should there be no flour on the table? Because the biggest mistake we can make when kneading is to use extra flour. That way, you just steadily incorporate more and more flour into your mix, thereby changing the recipe and the consistency of your bread. Too much flour can make bread very dense and unappetising. Extra flour at this early stage can give a very misleading sense of comfort and security.

Stretch and work the dough

Still using the hand involved in bringing the dough together (it will be beyond salvation by now: very sticky and doughy from bringing the ingredients together), stretch the dough fully away from you on the work surface. You can use your other hand to hold the bottom part of the dough to stop it from moving all over the place. Use the heel of your kneading hand rather than the palm for a more effective action. Don't hesitate to be over-dramatic when stretching the dough, and don't be afraid to elongate it. Even if it breaks, it doesn't matter; your gluten will mend and your dough will come back together. Now fold that piece of dough back onto itself and stretch it again. Occasionally rotate your dough so that it is kneaded from every angle. If your dough is very wet, as for a ciabatta or a focaccia, use only one hand at all times.

During kneading, use your scraper to bring your dough together at regular intervals. You'll observe that the scraper is doing a pretty good job at rounding up all the bits of dough on the table without having to use extra flour. Stretch ... fold ... stretch ... fold ... scrape ... rotate ... stretch ... fold ... stretch ... , and so on, will be your mantra for the next 6–8 minutes (and no more than 10 minutes). All this should be done at pace. The slower your kneading, the stickier your dough will become. If your hands get sticky, just stop and rub them over the dough until most of the bits are gone. Your hands will still be covered by a thin layer of dough, but that will dry in no time, making your hands essentially unsticky when you begin to knead again. Use your dough like a sponge to incorporate all the bits that have fallen off your hands, then continue with your mantra: Stretch ... fold ... stretch ... fold ... scrape ... rotate ... stretch ... fold ... stretch ... , and so on.

The folding technique

You can alter your kneading technique by switching to folding the dough towards yourself, rolling it away from you, then rotating it; fold it towards you once more, then begin again. You're using the weight of your body to do the hard work for you. You can also slap the dough on the table, as if beating a club on the surface, stretching your dough more and more – although take care not to have a piece of dough detach itself and fly through the kitchen! You can make use of all these techniques during your kneading session. Turn it into a health-giving workout – a therapeutic and liberating experience.

These different techniques all have in common the main purpose of kneading, which is: elongating the dough, thereby developing the gluten in the dough to give stretchability in your loaf when you come to shape it later on. Also, that tight, elastic gluten matrix will trap the CO_2 from the fermentation, and later the steam from your loaf when it is baking.

Gather the dough into a ball

The final step, when you have finished kneading, is to turn your dough into a round ball. You do this by placing both hands on the sides of your dough and rotating them together with the dough on the same spot; once again, no additional flour is required. What you're doing at this point is giving your dough some tension and structure immediately after kneading. It should not be a shapeless, limp piece of dough that gets casually tossed into the bowl, but a structured piece of dough placed with respect in the bowl. Always cover your dough when it is proving (see the next section) to prevent it from forming a crust, which would be detrimental to the development of your dough.

TIP
To avoid having to go to the sink every time your hands get a bit sticky, have a small bowl of flour nearby in which you can rub your hands until they are free of dough. They might feel a bit crusty, but you can still work with crusty hands as you move on to the next dough, or job. You can dip your hard-working (and doughy) scraper in the flour for a quick rub as well.

Kneading is such a crucial stage in your journey from initial ingredients to finished loaf of bread, which is why I have described it in as much detail as possible.

Proving

With your kneading done and dusted, the next fundamental step begins: proving.

While your dough is proving, the gluten will relax as it recovers from the strenuous kneading action that your hands have inflicted on the dough. At the same time, the yeast will begin its work of leavening by feeding on the natural sugar brought to it by the enzyme activity that is transforming the starch in the flour into simple sugars, making them accessible to the yeast. In baking, we tend to focus on the yeast and forget that without the enzymes in the flour there would be no fermentation. The enzymes act as catalysts, precipitating changes in ingredients and turning them into something else – they are the true transformers. If there are no enzymes there will be no fermented bread.

Managing the fermentation process

Your job as a baker is to make sure that you are looking after that fermentation process, that you're ensuring that it lasts and that it peaks all through the process, first after kneading (this is called the 'first rise' or 'bulk fermentation'), and second when the dough has been shaped into a loaf (the 'second rise').

Too long a fermentation, either during the first or second rise, means that the yeast would already be exhausted when it is still needed to produce a nice plump loaf. The result would be a flat, collapsed bread with a dense, almost cake-like crumb.

Too short a fermentation for the first or second rise will affect the dough's development, stopping it when it should actually have gone on for much longer. If this happens, when baked, the loaf will have the very round, bloated aspect of a grossly under-proved bread with a tight crumb.

What you need to achieve is a sort of balancing act between the fermentation across those two rises to be certain that there will still be some energy left in the dough when you put your bread in the oven. Understanding fermentation, and therefore respecting proving times, is crucial for producing a perfect loaf. But don't worry, we will go over proving times in each recipe. Not all loaves ferment in the same way.

Slowing fermentation through chilling

You can delay your dough's fermentation – and I would encourage you to do so when you have become more familiar with the recipes – by using your fridge. At about 4°C or 5°C, your dough will be at a much lower temperature than the kitchen and will remain nearly dormant. As a result, it will ferment very slowly, without over-proving. A longer fermentation in a controlled environment will help you to make much better bread that is full of flavour. If you do opt for a long, cold fermentation, you should still initiate the fermentation at room temperature for anything from 45 minutes to two hours, depending on the type of bread and fermentation. A sourdough fermentation, for example, is much slower than that for a dough made with fresh or dried yeast, and it will need more time at room temperature before being placed in the fridge.

Avoiding a crust while proving

When proving a dough, always remember to cover it. A draughty kitchen will definitely cause a crust to form on the outside of the loaf, which will hinder its full development. At home, I use a loose plastic bag. A shower cap is good to have as part of your baking paraphernalia; you can use it time and time again without battling with single-use plastic wrap, or, even more environmentally friendly, just use a plate placed over the bowl or a proving basket. For the latter, a deeper dish might be better, as you still need a bit of height to accommodate the increase in volume of the loaf during proving. Beeswax food wraps can also be a very good alternative. I have found that covering the dough with a tea towel, at whatever stage it is at in its journey, will not prevent a crust from forming because the textile is too porous to effectively seal off the dough from the surrounding air. In baking, all these little practical – almost trivial – details are very important.

THE BEST TEMPERATURE FOR PROVING

The recipes call for a 'warm place' to prove your dough. The ambient temperature in the kitchen will be fine as long as it is 24–25°C, or perhaps you might have a warmer spot in the kitchen if it is quite cold.

PROVING IN THE OVEN

I sometimes turn my electric fan oven into a makeshift prover by lowering it to 30°C (unfortunately a gas oven cannot go to a low enough temperature) – no more than that because anything higher than 50°C will kill your yeast. I spray water on the side of the oven chamber to create humidity, then I leave my dough to prove for 15–20 minutes. I then switch the oven off and leave the dough inside – the temperature will slowly be lowering without threatening my fermentation. (Alternatively, you could take the dough out of the oven after 15–20 minutes and leave it at room temperature to finish fermenting gently.)

Shaping

After kneading, the dough goes through the first rise (or bulk fermentation), during which the yeast leavens your dough, making it puffy as the yeast feeds on the starch, which is being transformed into simple sugars thanks to the help of the enzymes contained in the flour. Without these enzymes, you would not have a loaf. The yeast is like us: it needs to breathe, and when it breathes out, it expels carbon dioxide. It also needs to feed and to reproduce, and all this contributes to the dough trapping more and more carbon dioxide into the gluten matrix, steadily increasing the overall volume of your dough.

The second process taking place during the bulk fermentation is that the gluten is relaxing and gaining more elasticity. The gluten carries on binding, further tightening its matrix, which began to develop during kneading.

The two stages of shaping

It is time now to structure our bread again, and this will happen during the shaping stage. Shaping can be divided into two actions: first, pre-shaping, followed by the shaping itself. Pre-shaping is done just after you have weighed your dough into the desired amounts for your loaves (that's if you're not planning on using all your dough to make one large loaf of bread). Instead of leaving each piece on the work surface as they were cut, you will guide them towards their intended final shape. In doing so, you are once again introducing some order into your budding loaves, by putting some gentle tension on the outside of the dough. Just bring the corners of the divided dough into the middle, rotating it a fraction each time.

After pre-shaping, leave the dough to relax – covered as always, to avoid a crust forming – for 10–15 minutes. This is called a 'bench-rest'. It gives the dough another opportunity to further develop before it is finally shaped, a kind of intermediate proving.

Final shaping is your last chance to structure your loaf before it is baked. You will be helped by the fact that you have already pre-shaped your loaf and will be simply continuing that preliminary work. At this point, you are aiming to bring further tension to your loaf to prevent it from being over-loose as it proves for a second time, which might result in a flatter loaf when it comes out of the oven.

Shaping will differ, depending on the intended appearance of your loaf: essentially round, or long. Whatever the desired shape, always try to shape the loaf without using any extra flour. If you simply have to add flour because the dough is too sticky, try to keep this to the absolute minimum. Shaping on a heavily floured table will definitely make your shaping much harder and you won't be able to seal your bread properly.

Round shapes

If you want a round loaf, pick up the dough after its bench-rest, place it in front of you, turn it over and fold it by bringing the outside of the dough to the middle, just going around it once.

That dough will now look like a gigantic dumpling with the outside pinched together in the middle. This wrinkly part is called the seam. By doing this, the excess gas in the loaf will be allowed to escape, but you will also be restarting the fermentation, which will be needed to sustain the second rise. Now, turn the loaf over once more, so that the seam is against the work surface. Use both hands to squeeze the seam by cupping your hands under the loaf and pressing both sides together firmly, then rotate your dough several times doing the same thing until the outside of the loaf is smooth and firm. To finish, rotate the dough on the same spot, holding it with both hands. The seam sticking to the work surface will help you to give the dough tension, thereby completing the shaping. Your bread is now ready to be put in a proving basket upside down, seam up – your bread will then be the right way up when placed on a wooden peel, or prepared baking sheet, prior to being placed in the oven.

Long shapes

For a long loaf, such as a baguette or a bloomer, the process is slightly different, even if the principles are the same. In this case, turn your loaf over after the bench-rest, seam upwards. Then press down gently on your loaf to allow the excess gas to escape and to restart the fermentation process. Now fold the loaf towards you, just enough to create a kind of fat lip. Repeat this once more and you'll notice that you don't have enough space to do it again, so just turn it over with the seam against the table (you will see a line running along your loaf – this is the seam). Place both your hands on the middle part of your loaf and, with a bit of pressure, extend your loaf outwards in a rocking, back-and-forth movement until it has attained the desired length. Your loaf is now ready for the long, floured proving basket or loaf tin, or tea towel (if making baguettes). The seam should be facing upwards unless you are putting your loaf in a tin, in which case the seam should be at the bottom of the tin.

I would advise you to get a couple of different shapes of proving baskets. Leaving a loaf to prove without support, will make it spread sideways, resulting in a flat loaf. If the loaf is constrained during proving, the power of fermentation is forced upwards; it is not dispersed by spreading in every direction.

Your loaf, or loaves, are now entering the second, and final, rise as a shaped product. The next stage is baking.

Baking

This is the moment you've been anticipating since the start! It seems easy: put your bread in the oven, close the door and wait ... but, like any other step in bread-making, don't treat it too casually. There are a few rules that need to be respected to achieve a successful bake.

Before baking you will obviously need to assess if your loaf is 'ripe' enough to be brought to the oven, and that is often when we go wrong. When we first start grappling with fermentation, we tend to under-prove or over-prove significantly. We have all heard somewhere that long fermentation brings more flavour than a shorter time, but, despite meaning well, we do not thoroughly understand the whole process. A good friend of mine, attempting to make sourdough bread, phoned me to ask me why her time-consuming loaf had gone so flat when she put it on a tray to bake it. When I asked her how long she had proved it for, she told me 12 hours ... in her drying cupboard! Unfortunately for her loaf, its yeast activity was long past its best. It had become an over-tired fermentation, with no energy or life left in the poor loaf. The gluten in the dough had begun almost to liquidise. As a result, it no longer held the shape of the loaf. The enzymes had sped up the deterioration of the gluten strands beyond recognition, so that the former allies in allowing fermentation in her bread had ended up destroying it: a Greek tragedy played out in the amphitheatre of her proving basket!

What to look for before baking

A healthy, happy loaf ready for the oven should still have a smooth exterior, without a crust, and a plump appearance (roughly doubled in size, at least level with, if not slightly over, the rim of your proving basket). When gently prodded, the dough should slowly bounce back, so that the indentation left by your finger gradually disappears. This shows that there is still yeast activity to allow for the final push of the loaf in the oven to achieve its final volume.

Once you have decided that your loaf is ready for the oven, you still need to deal with it with care, as rough handling of an oven-ready loaf could cause it to deflate. Using a tray or a peel to deposit the bread onto a baking stone, you need to take the loaf out of the proving basket with caution by tilting one side of the basket with one hand while cushioning its fall with the other. If the loaf is stuck to the sides of the basket – and this can easily happen when your loaf has been left to ferment overnight in the fridge, don't pull it out too energetically: tease it out very gently with your fingers. This should enable you to safely retrieve the loaf you have already put so much effort into.

Scoring

The bread, once out of the proving basket, must now be scored. Many bakers consider slashing their bread to be their personal, professional signature. Apart from this, scoring a loaf fulfils two important functions: firstly, it can be done to create a decorative pattern, making the loaf more attractive, and more likely to be bought; secondly, and probably more importantly, scoring enables steam to escape in an orderly way. As mentioned earlier, when your bread bakes it boils, turning into a pressure cooker and producing steam that has to escape. The baker, anticipating this, creates vents on the outside of the loaf to allow the steam to escape in an orderly, rather than a chaotic, way. Without scoring, the steam would simply find the weakest points in the loaf, which might result in a misshapen loaf, or cause unsightly cracks in the bread. The baker, therefore, artificially creates weak points through which the steam can escape without causing damage.

To score the loaf, it is better to use a razor blade than a knife. However sharp your knife, its blade will always be thicker and less sharp than a razor blade. A knife might well end up deflating your loaf, whereas a razor blade will enable a more precise slashing action, almost like a surgical cut, on your bread with far less risk of damaging the dough. When you score the bread, don't use the whole length of the blade as if you are ploughing through the bread, just use a corner of the blade. Because your blade has four corners, you can keep using it for quite some time before having to change it for a brand-new one.

Producing steam for the perfect bake

Now that it has been scored, the loaf is ready for baking. It is vitally important that at this moment sufficient steam is produced to caramelise the crust. No steam, no joy, I say. Two things will be happening in your oven: (1) the gluten in your loaf will be coagulating: being a protein, the gluten will set as a result of the action of the heat, and then harden; and (2) the natural sugars on the outside of the bread will caramelise when in contact with the steam (remember the catalytic action of enzymes transforming the starch in the flour into simple sugars and thereby inducing fermentation). Not enough steam, or no steam at all, will turn the crust greyish and dull, a colour unattractive to the eye. Also, the humidity created by the steam produced in your oven will help with the last development of volume in your loaf. It will be much more likely to bloom happily in a very hot and humid oven.

There are two different methods to produce steam. The simplest is if your oven has a steam function, which you have totally forgotten about (or you didn't know that it had). Otherwise, you can spray water against the side of the oven (making sure that you don't spray the loaves themselves). Always close the oven door quickly after putting your loaf in to avoid losing the steam. This is an efficient way of producing steam, but if the water where you live is hard, limescale might start to develop on the sides of your oven, though you could always wipe the oven with a cloth dampened with white wine vinegar to get rid of it, which is not too time-consuming. Alternatively, you can produce steam by placing a tray in the oven prior to baking until it is really hot, then throwing in just enough chilled water to cover the tray. The thermal shock of the very cold water on the very hot tray will immediately transform the water into steam.

Whichever method you're using, your aim is to create an abundant amount of steam. Your domestic oven is not a baker's oven, so there won't be enough steam produced and, equally importantly, kept efficiently inside. What is lacking in a domestic oven is the self-containment effect present in a professional deck oven where numerous loaves are sitting tightly side by side producing an enormous amount of steam by themselves, which helps with the caramelisation of the crust, giving that lovely shine you get on a professionally produced loaf. In order to replicate that self-containment effect as closely as possible, you have to almost over-steam your oven at the beginning of baking, knowing that you can always dry your bread by opening the oven door 5 minutes before the end of baking to let the surplus steam escape, if need be. Leave the door slightly ajar for just 30 seconds or so, taking care not to place your face too near the door; steam is hotter than boiling water and will definitely give you some nasty burns. Baking several loaves, rather than a single lonely loaf, and making use of the whole space available in your oven, will also help with a better baking session.

Light or dark crust – which is best?

What colour should that crust be? Don't stop at the traditional golden look. Come and join us on the 'dark side', where all real bread bakers live. I nicknamed myself the Prince of Darkness (the original Prince of Darkness is the great Sim Cass, former baker extraordinaire at the famous Balthazar Bakery in New York, who I had the pleasure to meet at the Bread Ahead Bakery School, and I totally share his take on the matter). The darker the better, especially with bigger loaves – you really want a contrast between the crust and the crumb. The slight bitterness of an overdone crust brings more flavour to the softer crumb. They complement each other and also increase the sensory properties of your bread, appealing to both taste and smell. Of course, some breads might need less drastic baking. I'm just trying to encourage a more adventurous mindset, to push the boundaries of what might seem an acceptable colour for your bread's crust.

When is your loaf cooked?

Finally, when your bread is ready, turn it over and tap it gently on the underside. If it gives a nice clear sound, a bit like a well-tuned drum, your loaf is baked. Transfer it immediately onto a wire rack to cool. Don't leave it on the tray or in the tin it has been baked in, as that would make it soft or even soggy on the bottom. Sit back and enjoy the sweet and uplifting sound of your bread cooling down. It is singing for the sole enjoyment of its creator!

All You Need to Know – in a Nutshell

Before we start with the recipes, let's summarise the key points so far. We've already covered a lot of ground, which might have been a bit overwhelming.

1 **Ingredients** Real bread-making involves just four basic ingredients: flour, water, yeast (or sourdough starter) and salt. (This is unless you want to enrich a dough, such as for a brioche.)

2 **Kneading** helps the gluten come together to trap the carbon dioxide from fermentation, and later on the steam produced during baking. To begin with, simply combine the ingredients in a bowl to form a loose dough. Transfer the dough from the bowl to your work surface.

3 **Scrape** the bowl clean to make the most of your dough and to ensure that your ingredients remain in the correct proportions.

4 **Don't add any extra flour** during kneading. Just use a bendy scraper to regroup the dough at regular intervals. Using the heel of your hand, stretch the dough as far as you reasonably can and fold it back onto itself, then repeat. Kneading by hand, or machine, should take only 6–10 minutes. Stretch your dough very delicately to check how the gluten is developing. If it feels elastic and is getting very

thin without breaking straight away, it means that your gluten matrix is sufficiently developed to fulfil its carbon dioxide trapping role.

5   **Finish your kneading by shaping** your dough into a round shape, then cover it. The first rise (or bulk fermentation) can now start; it will gather momentum and begin to develop the structure of your bread.

6   **Proving occurs in three phases:** the first rise, bench-rest, and the second rise. The proving time will vary according to the type of fermentation and the quantity of yeast used in the recipe; for example, a sourdough bread will take longer to ferment than a bread made with yeast. Follow the proving time suggested in the recipe, but remember that a temperature of 24 or 25°C is considered the best temperature for leavening bread, so bear this in mind, as a cooler or hotter environment will alter those times. Successful proving depends on nurturing the fermentation right up to when the bread goes in the oven to ensure that the yeast is still active and not already declining in strength.

7   **Shaping is structuring** Before shaping, you need to pre-shape your loaf by giving it the rough appearance of the final product. Pre-shaping is followed by what we call a bench-rest: an important stage that allows the loaf to gently replace the CO_2 expelled during pre-shaping and the gluten to relax. The final step is shaping, when your loaf takes on its definitive form: your last chance to structure your loaf before its second rise. This is a crucial stage, as sloppy shaping will not deliver the goods at the end of your baking day.

8   **Scoring will give your loaf an attractive look** and it will allow the steam that builds up inside the bread to come out in an orderly fashion. Use a razor blade, not a knife; a razor blade will cut through the surface of the loaf with more precision and less effort than the relatively thick blade of a knife. Use only one corner of the razor blade, not the whole edge, as that way you might plough through the dough and spoil both the look and the quality of your loaf.

9   **Baking a loaf will always require a much higher temperature** than pastries, for example, so it is very important that your oven is pre-heated to the desired temperature at least 30 minutes before putting your bread in. Generally speaking, the temperature should be 230–250°C. You can always lower the temperature after a while for your bread to carry on baking in a less harsh heat.

10   **Don't bake your loaf without steaming** as you're loading it in the oven. Heat will coagulate the gluten, creating the crust, and the steam will colour the crust through the caramelisation of the natural sugars covering the outside of your loaf. Steam will also produce a humid environment and, through the combination of a mighty heat and high humidity, it will allow further expansion of the loaf: that desirable oven 'bloom'.

11   **A thoroughly baked bread will sound hollow** when out of the oven. Tap the underside of the loaf with your fingers several times and listen out for a nice crisp, clear sound.

These are just a few points in summary to keep in mind as you get stuck into the recipes. Now, let's get started!

Ingredients

Let's look at the four basic ingredients that we will be using in the following recipes. I won't go into too much detail, because there is a lot of information out there available for you to research, if you want to, which will go into much more detail. These are the bare essentials, to ensure that you're not drowning in unnecessary technical knowledge.

Flour

For bread making it is important to have the higher ratio of gluten in hard-wheat flours than is found in soft flours, which are generally used for pastry. A good, strong white flour starts at around 12 per cent gluten going up to 18 per cent, as in the case of Canadian wheat, which is wheat on steroids! Gluten is the protein in the flour, which is going to bind progressively, transforming into a matrix with a tight mesh, trapping most of the CO_2 from the fermentation and the steam from the baking to give volume to your loaf.

For pastry, you don't need much gluten because developing it isn't that important. On the contrary, too much gluten could lead to tough pastry dough when you are after a more crumbly, more brittle quality.

Wholemeal flour is made out of the whole of the wheat grain. It is considered far more nutritious than white flour because it retains both the bran and the wheatgerm – the fat reserve of the grain. These are not left behind in the milling stage as they are with white flour. White flour is mostly starch, which is transformed into natural sugars during fermentation. This is why people with diabetes should move away from white bread and turn to wholemeal bread with its slow-releasing sugars. Used on its own it will give quite a dense texture. It is better for the sake of lightness when making bread to combine strong wholemeal flour with some strong white flour.

Spelt and ancient wheat such as Khorasan (also known as kamut), emmer, farro or einkorn are primitive crops that haven't been extensively changed, like modern wheat. Healthy and nutritious, they have however a fairly fragile gluten, which means that they are highly digestible and gentle on the stomach. The downside is that they are a bit tricky to work with. We'll discuss this later in the book.

Rye is another healthy cereal with a very distinct flavour. It is a great favourite in Northern and Eastern baking, and rightly so. It should be treated like an ancient grain and does not require extensive kneading. If you can get hold of light or medium rye, that will make your loaf less dense than using 100 per cent dark rye. Or you could always sieve your dark rye to turn it into a much lighter version.

Water

You don't have to use mineral water in your bread. I've been working in bakeries for 25 years and I've never seen a pallet of Evian water bottles next to a mixer. Just occasionally a tin of beer perhaps . . . Like every professional baker in the land, use tap water.

I would rather spend more time getting the temperature of my water right. Baking books rarely mention this very significant factor in making bread. Water acts like a corrective to your environment. The best temperature for fermentation is 24.6°C (but 24 or 25°C will do) and this is exactly the water temperature that's going to take you there. You can't warm up your kitchen or your flour quickly, but on the contrary it is very simple to change the temperature of the water at the sink.

As a rule of thumb, if your kitchen is cold, your flour will also be cold (even slightly cooler, as the flour will store the ambient temperature more efficiently). Adding cold water would therefore result in a cold dough, slowing down the yeast and preventing sufficient dough development. Using warmer water in the mix will raise the temperature of your dough towards the perfect temperature range of 24–25°C. If your kitchen is quite warm, the process should be the opposite. Cold water will be necessary this time to lower the temperature of the dough towards 24–25°C. In good artisanal bakeries, at the start of the working day, the head baker will take the temperature of the bakery and the temperature of the flour before deciding on the temperature of the water for the mix. Remember: a baker bakes in line with his or her environment.

> **ALWAYS ADJUST YOUR WATER TEMPERATURE**
>
> Remember, when adding water, always adjust to your environment and follow your gut feeling. If your kitchen is hot or cold, your flour will also be hot or cold, which means that your water should be the opposite to counterbalance the environment. Your water could be warm or cold, or even chilled, on a very hot summer's day. Generally speaking, your water should be warm, or warmish, in the winter and cold or even chilled in the summer.

Salt

When making the recipes in this book, try to use natural, fine sea salt, because table (or cooking) salt usually includes additional chemicals to prevent the salt from clumping as a result of moisture. The sodium or potassium ferrocyanide used for this doesn't seem like a great ingredient to put in your bread. If using flakes of sea salt, such as Maldon, grind this using a pestle and mortar until it is fine. But if you can't find the natural stuff, don't postpone your baking session. You can use table salt if necessary, with my blessing.

Salt has three roles in baking:

1   First, the obvious one: it seasons the bread, giving it taste.

2   It puts the brakes on the fermentation because salt in direct contact with yeast will end up killing it, even after just a short while, and as a baker you are using that effect to your advantage: you are controlling the fermentation by delaying it.

3   It hardens the gluten strands in the dough thereby helping to create the overall structure of your loaf. If you forget to use salt, your bread will be flat – guaranteed!

Yeast

Commercial fresh and dried yeast are simply the same type of yeast and are needed to provide fermentation. They are packed with a selected species of fungus commonly called baker's yeast (*Saccharomyces cerevisiae*), which transforms carbohydrates into alcohol and CO_2, the two by-products of fermentation.

Fresh yeast needs to be kept in the fridge and has a limited shelf life of 2–3 weeks. Dried yeast is far more flexible: it can be stored at room temperature and even with the tin open it will still be active for months. It is always important to read the instructions on the sachet or the side of the tin to know which type of dried yeast you're dealing with. There are two types, dried yeast and fast-action/easy-bake dried yeast:

Dried active yeast will need to be dissolved in water to be activated before adding to the rest of the ingredients.

Fast action/easy-bake dried yeast is already activated and can be mixed directly with the flour. We use this yeast in the recipes.

Dried yeast is more potent than fresh yeast, so you will have to reduce the amount of dried yeast by half any amount of fresh yeast indicated in a recipe.

FRESH AND DRIED ACTIVE YEAST

Fast action/easy-bake dried yeast is used in the recipes but you can use the other types of yeast if you wish. Here's how:

To use fresh yeast Use twice the quantity stated for fast action/easy-bake dried yeast. Crumble the yeast into the flour and follow the recipe as stated.

To use dried active yeast Use the same quantity of dried active yeast as given in the recipe for fast-action/easy-bake dried yeast. Put the yeast into a small bowl and add 50ml water from the quantity given in the recipe (check the water temperature as explained on page 49). Stir, then leave it for 5 minutes or until frothy. Add this mixture to the flour and add the remaining water as stated in the recipe.

A note on the use of sugar Usually in baking books, sugar is mentioned as necessary to stimulate fermentation (and it will indeed), but there are already some sugars waiting in our flour to feed our fermentation. I would rather rely on a natural fermentation rather than add processed white sugar unnecessarily to my bread.

Essential Equipment

For me, baking will always be cheap and cheerful in essence, and it should stay positively low-tech. There is no need to spend loads of money. Here is the equipment that I consider essential.

Kitchen scales

You haven't yet reached the stage when you can guess quantities, so kitchen scales are strongly recommended. Digital scales are more precise and you should weigh even your liquids for more accuracy.

LIQUID MEASUREMENTS
All the measurements in the recipes, even for liquids, will be in grams (g) for greater accuracy but I have given millilitres (ml) as well in case you have a different kind of kitchen scale.

Mixing bowls

These can be made of plastic, wood, ceramic or metal – it really doesn't matter – but make sure that they're not too small so that you can make bigger batches of bread in one go if necessary.

Scraper

This is an absolutely indispensable tool for baking. Soon it will become just a normal extension of your hand. You can clean your bowl, or your work surface, cut the dough, spread a filling, shape a loaf or, more importantly, use it to help you knead, avoiding the use of extra flour, which could completely change your loaf, as explained on page 24.

Proving baskets

You can find some cheap ones online made out of wood – in both round and long shapes. They're no gimmick; they are actually critical in keeping the dough in the intended shape right up to baking time. In the meantime, however, a mixing bowl lined with a tea towel would be totally fine.

Knives, forks and spoons

A small table knife and a bigger cook's knife will do. A few tablespoons and teaspoons (even the odd fork) are always handy.

Cutters

For puff pastry, shortbreads, scones, biscuits, cookies, used in general baking, but not for breadmaking.

Electric stand mixer

For a few of the recipes in the book it would help, although it is not essential, to have an electric stand mixer. With enriched doughs, butter needs to be incorporated very quickly before it melts, and an electric mixer can help with this.

Recipes

Italian Breads

Let's start your baking journey with a small, carefully chosen selection of recipes. This limited number of recipes is entirely intentional. The aim is not to overwhelm you with too many different kinds of bread. My feeling is that it is much better for you to master these simple recipes, as they will give you the basic techniques to then move on to explore other more comprehensive or specialised baking books. These are a starting point, the first ferments to leaven your interest in baking.

CIABATTA

An Italian classic, the ciabatta is one of three recipes, alongside the focaccia and the grissini, that will create a Mediterranean feel at your dinner table and take centre stage. Ciabatta is an easy, friendly bread for the novice, as there is no real shaping involved. The main challenge is in our ability to deal with a 'sticky situation'. Beware: the dough will be very soft; some might find it disconcerting, off-putting even, but I would urge you to persevere, because the reward will be well worth any initial trouble. This recipe uses an all-in-one-bowl technique, like the rest of the recipes (it's much more convenient than multiple bowls to hold different ingredients).

4g fast-action/easy-bake dried yeast

800g strong white flour, plus extra for dusting

12g natural fine sea salt

extra virgin olive oil, for greasing

200g stoned green or black olives
(or use a mixture of the two) (optional)

semolina or polenta, for sprinkling

You will need:

2 baking sheets

1
Put your mixing bowl on the scales and set it to 0g, then measure the yeast. Set the scale back to 0g before measuring the next ingredient. Add 700g/700ml water to the bowl. (Adjust the temperature of the water according to your kitchen environment.)

2
Set the scale back to 0g, then add the flour. Put the bowl to one side and weigh the salt separately in a small bowl on the scales. (This makes it easier to correct in case you add too much on top of the other ingredients.) Add to the bowl with the flour.

3

Using only one hand, mix the ingredients together until they form a loose dough – there should be no flour lurking at the bottom or on the sides of your bowl. All your ingredients must be fully combined. At that moment the dough will feel very wet, like a thick batter. Holding the bowl firmly with the other (clean) hand, start making a simple kneading action; whip the dough energetically round and round in a circular movement for about 5 minutes. The dough should look quite smooth and more stretchy than when you began kneading.

4

Slowly pour some oil around the dough – just enough to stop the dough from sticking to the bowl. Then push down the oil under the dough using your scraper around the bowl.

5

It is now time to fold the ciabatta for a bit more structure. Add the olives now, if you're using them. Take one side of the dough and bring it into the middle of the bowl, repeat with the opposite side. Rotate the bowl and start again, bringing one side towards the middle and then the other side. When the dough has been folded in the middle, just turn it over. This whole action is called a fold. The folding process will incorporate the olives.

6

Cover your ciabatta with a shower cap or plastic bag and put it aside in a warm place to prove for 45–60 minutes until roughly doubled in size.

7

Repeat the folding process twice with the same resting time between folding of 45–60 minutes.

8

Fold the dough again for a fourth time, but instead of turning it over in the bowl, turn it over onto a heavily floured work surface to prevent it sticking to the surface. (Although generally we want to avoid adding extra flour, in this case, with such a wet dough, flour is necessary.) Dust the top of the ciabatta with flour and cover it. Leave it to rest for 20 minutes.

9

Preheat the oven to 240°C (220°C fan oven) Gas 9. Sprinkle the baking sheets with semolina. Divide the dough into four equal strips using the non-curved side of your scraper, making sure that you cut through the ciabatta right down to the work surface. Pull each section away from the main body of dough to avoid them sticking back together. Handle the ciabattas very carefully to avoid deflating them: slide both hands under the ciabatta squeezing it slightly and transfer it to the prepared baking sheets, putting two ciabatta on each sheet. (Alternatively, to make panini, divide each ciabatta into two or three equal pieces and transfer to the baking sheets.)

10

Spray the sides of the oven chamber to create steam. Bake the loaves for 16–18 minutes until golden brown and when you tap on the base it sounds hollow, or you can aim for a darker colour if you like. Your loaves will become soft when cooled. Transfer to a wire rack to cool.

FOCACCIA

A staple of Italian baking, focaccia uses a folding technique in the same way as ciabatta (on page 63) to make it a structurally strong and to avoid it deflating during handling before it goes into the oven. Enjoy focaccia dipped in yet more olive oil (there's a lot in the recipe itself) or in pesto, baba ghanoush, tzatziki, spicy tomato dip or even a cold ratatouille. Whichever way you eat it, it really is exceptionally good – the type of bread that offers an instant reward.

MAKES 1 HEFTY 900G FOCACCIA, ENOUGH TO FEED THE WHOLE FAMILY OR A NUMBER OF FRIENDS!

3g fast-action/easy-bake dried yeast

450g strong white flour

8g natural fine sea salt

50g/50ml extra virgin olive oil, plus extra for brushing

toppings of your choice, such as sliced tomatoes, sliced olives, grated cheese, fresh rosemary or thyme leaves, roasted garlic or sliced onion

You will need:

small, deep baking tray (a large one will do; just keep the focaccia in the middle of the tray)

1

Put your mixing bowl on the scales and set it to 0g, then measure the yeast. Set the scale back to 0g before measuring the next ingredient. Add 360g/360ml water to the bowl. (Adjust the temperature of the water according to your kitchen.)

2

Set the scale back to 0g, then add the flour. Put the bowl to one side and weigh the salt separately in a small bowl on the scales. (This makes it easier to correct in case you add too much on top of the other ingredients.) Add to the bowl with the flour.

3

Using only one hand, mix the ingredients together until they form a loose dough – there should be no flour lurking at the bottom or on the sides of the bowl. All your ingredients must be fully combined. At that moment the dough will feel very wet, like a thick batter. Holding the bowl firmly with the other (clean) hand, begin a simple kneading motion: whip the dough energetically in a circular movement for about 5 minutes. The dough should be looking quite smooth and should be more stretchy than when you began kneading.

4

Slowly pour the olive oil around the dough. It will look as if it is swimming in it, but don't worry. All that golden goodness is going to be incorporated into the dough through the folding process. Now push down the oil by using your scraper to scrape down the sides of the bowl around the dough.

5

It is now time to fold the focaccia for a bit more structure. What's going to happen when you fold it is that you are going to gently laminate the dough, creating layers of oil and air, which will benefit the overall structure and fermentation of the bread. Take one side of the dough and bring it in to the middle of the bowl, then repeat with the opposite side. Rotate the bowl and start again, bringing one side towards the middle and then the other side. When the dough has been folded into the middle, just turn it over. This whole action is called a fold.

6

Cover your focaccia with a shower cap or plastic bag and put it aside in a warm place to prove for 45–60 minutes until roughly doubled in size. There is not much yeast in this recipe, so it might be necessary to leave it to ferment for slightly longer.

7

Repeat the folding process twice, resting the dough between folding for 45–60 minutes.

8

Preheat the oven to 240°C (220°C fan oven) Gas 9 and line a small, deep baking tray with baking paper. Fold the dough for a fourth time, but instead of turning the dough over in the bowl, turn it over into the prepared baking tray. Pour any olive oil left in the bowl over the focaccia. Spread the dough to more or less cover the tray using your fingers, then leave it to rest for 20 minutes (oil will protect the dough from crusting).

9

Add the toppings of your choice. Just remember not to overload your focaccia with too many ingredients (an excess of tomatoes, in particular, will make it very soggy). Sometimes less is more!

10

Spray the sides of the oven chamber to create steam. Bake for 15–20 minutes until golden brown, or you can allow focaccia to bake until it is quite dark if you like. The dough contains a lot of water and olive oil, so it will be soft when cooled.

11

Put the tin on a wire rack, then carefully transfer the focaccia from the tin to the rack. Brush it generously with even more olive oil. How much? Well, how much do you love oil? There's never enough, I say!

GRISSINI

This is a northern Italian recipe, with Turin being considered the birthplace of grissini. It uses polenta (cornmeal), which is not altogether surprising since corn was cultivated in the Po valley in northern Italy when first it was brought back from the Americas in the 16th century. Corn rapidly found its way into the traditional northern Italian cooking and baking repertoire: in polenta, for example, the most popular dish in the region, and in sweet polenta cake. Given its dryness, grissini is perfect as an aperitif or starter. The corn element provides a pleasing crunch and texture. This version is truer to the original than those dreadful commercially produced, biscuit-style grissini, the staple of any rough-and-ready drinks party, full of ingredients such as sugar, palm oil and skimmed milk that are not a part of this traditional food.

I discovered grissini when I was invited to Turin many moons ago by the bread writer Dan Lepard to join the Salone di Gusto part of the Slow Food movement. I was billeted in a small bakery in the suburbs of the city where they were making grissini all day long. That bakery was a truly special place. The bakers ranged from old to very old. – it was an odd combination of working bakery, retirement home and a kind of Buena Vista Social Club! Red wine was also very much a part of the scene, which meant that by the end of the week my near non-existent Italian had come along remarkably.

This is a great bread to make with children. They can knead (and not for too long), shape, bake and then eat the grissini straight away, without having to wait for any fermentation to take place.

MAKES 14 GRISSINI

2g fast-action/easy-bake dried yeast

250g strong white flour

3g natural fine sea salt

20g polenta or semolina,
plus extra for kneading and sprinkling

olive oil, for brushing

3 tsp fresh chopped herbs, such as rosemary,
thyme or oregano (or use dried herbs)

1 tsp dried chilli flakes

sea salt flakes, for sprinkling

You will need:

baking sheet

1

Put your mixing bowl on the scales and set it to 0g, then measure the yeast. Set the scale back to 0g before measuring the next ingredient. Add 165g/165ml water to the bowl. (The temperature isn't important here, as there is no proving involved.)

2

Set the scale back to 0g, then add the flour, polenta, herbs and chilli flakes. Stir together to mix. Put the bowl to one side and weigh the salt separately in a small bowl on the scales. (This makes it easier to correct in case you add too much on top of the other ingredients.) Add to the bowl with the flour.

3

Using only one hand and a circular movement, bring together the ingredients to form a dough. This dough will feel quite firm. Put the dough on the work surface and, using the heel of your mixing hand, stretch it and fold it, or roll it back onto itself, then repeat the process, rotating the dough regularly to ensure that all the dough has been thoroughly kneaded. You really don't need to do this for very long: 3 or 4 minutes at most. You do not need to develop the gluten as much as for other fully structured breads; all you want are some nice little crunchy, skinny breadsticks. When bringing the dough together, throw in a handful of extra polenta to add some texture.

Cut the dough into roughly 30g pieces. They shouldn't be any bigger than that or the grissini might become too chewy. There is no need to make them into small balls; just use the palm of one hand to put some pressure on each piece and roll it on the work surface until it is long enough to be able to put the fingers of both hands together, side by side, on top of the grissini. Applying more pressure, extend the dough outwards from the middle until it reaches 35–40cm in length. (Don't use any flour during the shaping, as it will make it much harder to control the stretching.)

5

When you have finished shaping all the grissini, throw some more polenta onto the work surface and roll the grissini in it to coat them.

6

Preheat the oven to 240°C (220°C fan oven) Gas 9 and cover a baking sheet with baking paper. Sprinkle some polenta onto the prepared baking sheet. Put the grissini lengthways on the baking sheet to make the most of the space. If they are a tiny bit too long for your baking sheet, curve them at one or both ends – it doesn't really matter – making them into either shepherd's crooks or old-fashioned handlebar moustaches. Brush them lightly with oil and sprinkle with sea salt flakes.

7

Spray the sides of the oven chamber to create steam. Bake for 12 minutes, until golden brown – you don't want them to be only light golden in colour, you are after crunch above all! If the ends of your grissini are singed, that is perfectly acceptable. Transfer to a wire rack to cool.

8

All you need to do now is put them into a medium-sized jar so that you can fan them out widely for serving. Another fancy idea you might try would be to shape them into big curves giving the impression of a 'bread octopus' with its tasty tentacles spilling out of the jar. This is definitely an Instagram moment for the social-media-savvy young (or not-so-young)!

VARIATION

If you like, you can roll the unbaked grissini in seeds or a mixture of seeds of your choice, such as sesame, poppy, cumin, linseed or caraway. Avoid larger seeds such as pumpkin or sunflower seeds, as they will be too chunky to stick to the dough.

Morning Treats

Here are a handful of great recipes to lift everyone's spirits at breakfast or brunch. I'm pretty sure that they will be making regular appearances in your household.

BAGELS

Honestly, you can't beat a freshly baked bagel straight from your oven and then sliced open to be packed with your favourite filling. This bagel recipe will definitely be as close as you can get to a traditional bagel that you might find in London's Brick Lane. To get the distinctive chewy texture, the bagels are poached in water before baking. Bagels are street food par excellence, so there is a need for them to be produced at speed to make them profitable. The whole process is relatively quick, including a minimum proving time.

MAKES 8 BAGELS

7g fast-action/easy-bake dried yeast

8g barley syrup

500g strong white flour, plus extra for dusting

8g natural fine sea salt

oil, for greasing

60g sugar

your choice of toppings, such as seeds (sesame, poppy, pumpkin, sunflower, nigella, linseed or chia), dried chilli flakes, dried onion and sea salt flakes

You will need:

baking sheet

1

Put your mixing bowl on the scales and set it to 0g, then measure the yeast. Set the scale back to 0g before measuring the next ingredient. Add the barley syrup to the mixing bowl. Add 290g/290ml water to the bowl. (The water can be at room temperature, or even cold, as the dough will not be fully proved.)

2

Set the scale back to 0g, then add the flour. Put the bowl to one side and weigh the salt separately in a small bowl on the scales. (This makes it easier to correct in case you add too much on top of the other ingredients.) Add to the bowl with the flour.

3

Using only one hand in a circular movement, bring together the ingredients to form a dough. It will feel quite firm. Put the dough on the work surface and, using the heel of your mixing hand, stretch it and fold it, or roll it back onto itself, then repeat the process, rotating the dough regularly to ensure that all the dough has been thoroughly kneaded. This should take about 6–8 minutes. Cover the dough with a shower cap or plastic bag and leave it in a warm place to prove for 45 minutes or until roughly doubled in size. This first rise is not that long, because under-proving, alongside the initial poaching and a relatively short baking time, will add to the chewiness of the bagel.

4

Transfer the dough to a sparsely floured work surface and divide it into eight 105g pieces. Roll each piece into a ball. Fold the edges of the dough into the centre, going around the dough once only. The wrinkly side is called the seam. Turn the ball over so that the seam is against the work surface, then, using the palm of your hand, elongate each ball into an oval shape, rocking it back and forth. Place the mixing bowl over the dough balls for a 5-minute bench-rest.

5

Now it is time to shape the bagels. Take one pre-shaped piece of dough and turn it over so that you can see the seam. Flatten it lightly with one hand and start folding it towards you halfway, creating something like a fat lip. Seal that fold with your fingertips and start once again, sealing it in the same way towards you. Turn it over so that the seam is against the work surface, then, with both hands, start stretching the dough outwards to a 25cm length. Apply some pressure at both ends to make them pointy. (This is very much like the process for shaping a classic baguette, so it's good practice for when you make your first baguette.) Working as if you were in a factory, turn each ball into a kind of mini-baguette. If any are shrinking, leave them to rest and then go back to the first one you shaped to get it to the right size. Keep going over them in order until they are all done.

6

The next step is to join the two ends of your bagel so that they overlap generously by 4–5cm. Press them down firmly where the ends cross so that they stick tightly together. It is important not to use any extra flour during the shaping, as the ends would then not stick together and would then come apart when placed in the hot water later in the process. If you *have* used extra flour, just wet one end of your bagel and that will help it to stick to the other end. Repeat for all the other bagels.

7

Put your thumb on the outside of the ring that you have just created on one of the bagels and your other fingers inside the ring. The palm of your hand should be covering the part of the bagel where the ends overlap. Then, firmly roll the bagel back and forth very quickly on the work surface. Your bagel is now sealed. Don't worry if you can see the join, that's how it should be: these are hand-made, baker's bagels, not the seamless versions, like gigantic Polo mints, sold in supermarkets.

8

Preheat the oven to 220°C (200°C fan oven) Gas 7. Line a baking sheet with baking paper and oil the paper. Pour boiling water into a large saucepan and return it to the boil, then reduce the heat to a simmer. Put the bagels on the prepared baking sheet, then take the sheet to the pan of hot water. Add the sugar to the pan and stir to dissolve it in the water. Drop the bagels carefully into the water; you will probably need to do this in batches. Leave to poach for 30 seconds, then turn them over using a large slotted spoon or spider, and poach for another 30 seconds. Lift the bagels out of the water using the slotted spoon, and put them back on the oiled paper. Take great care during this poaching phase!

9

Sprinkle the toppings of your choice over the bagels. Spray the sides of the oven chamber to create steam, then bake the bagels for 15 minutes or until golden. You don't want to over-bake these in pursuit of a nice, dark colour all over. In the case of bagels, they would dry out and have a very limited shelf life. Don't forget, too, that your bagel is likely to go back in the oven, or in a toaster or under the grill at some point. Put them on a wire rack, and enjoy them when they are slightly cooler, perhaps simply with a dab of American mustard. Delicious!

ENGLISH MUFFINS

An English muffin makes a lovely breakfast. I always associate them a rasher of bacon, a poached egg and lashings of Hollandaise sauce from my time working at The Quality Chop House under the maverick Charles Fontaine, the ex-head chef at Le Caprice, who taught me so much about cooking. I remember those formative years with 'Charlot' with great fondness!

MAKES 9 MUFFINS

7g fast-action/easy-bake dried yeast

130g/130ml full fat or semi-skimmed milk,
at room temperature

320g strong white flour, plus extra for dusting

130g plain white flour

50g unsalted butter, softened, cut into pieces

1 tsp caster sugar

8g natural fine sea salt

semolina, for coating

You will need:

2 baking sheets

1

Put your mixing bowl on the scales and set it to 0g, then measure
the yeast. Set the scale back to 0g before measuring the next
ingredient. Add the milk and 130g/130ml water to the bowl.
(Adjust the temperature of the water according to your kitchen
environment.)

2

Set the scale back to 0g, then add the flours and sugar, setting the scale back to 0g before adding each. Set the scale back to 0g, then add the butter.

3

Put the bowl to one side and weigh the salt separately in a small bowl on the scales. (This makes it easier to correct in case you add too much on top of the other ingredients.) Add to the bowl with the flour mixture.

4

Using only one hand in a circular movement, bring the ingredients together to form a dough. It will feel quite firm. Put the dough on the table and, using your mixing hand, stretch it and fold it, or roll it back onto itself, then repeat the process, rotating the dough regularly to ensure that all the dough has been thoroughly kneaded. This should take 4–5 minutes at the most; you don't want to over-develop the gluten in this dough. Cover the dough with a shower cap or plastic bag and leave it in a warm place to prove for 45 minutes or until roughly doubled in size. English muffins don't need a long fermentation. This is an enriched dough with a fair amount of yeast, so the dough will develop quite quickly through the process.

5

Tip the dough out onto a lightly floured work surface. Divide it into nine 85g pieces, then pre-shape these into rounds and bench-rest for 5 minutes.

6

Line a baking sheet with baking paper. Shape the balls into round roll shapes. Dip the top and bottom of each muffin in semolina and put them on the prepared baking sheet, making sure that they're not too close to one another as they will spread with the weight of the other baking sheet that will be placed on top. Press them down slightly, then cover again as before and leave them in a warm place to prove for 20–30 minutes until roughly doubled in size.

7

Preheat the oven to 200°C (180°C fan oven) Gas 6. Put another sheet of baking paper over the muffins and then put the second baking sheet on top to keep them flat while cooking. Spray the sides of the oven chamber to create steam. Bake the muffins for 15–20 minutes until light golden on the top and bottom, remembering that they will be toasted later on, which will give them more colour.

8

Transfer to a wire rack, slice them open while still warm and spread on a generous amount of fabulously creamy English butter!

Flatbreads

This is probably the most ancient and efficient way of producing bread. All you need is an open fire, a stone or a sheet of metal placed over it and you can very quickly produce masses of bread. It is always impressive to see the speed with which bakers make mountains of lavash bread in very basic settings. Fresh from the oven, these flatbreads are truly delicious served with meze or used to wrap healthy fillings. And, as I usually say when teaching, with these breads, folks, we are in a win–win situation: what could go flatter than a flatbread? Although even that is a blatant lie, because there is nothing more depressing than a pitta that doesn't want to puff . . .

I have chosen two classic flatbreads: pitta and lavash. The first one needs no introduction. I'm sure we've all had a greasy kebab late on a Saturday night or in the wee hours of Sunday morning after a joyous pub session at some point in our life! As for the second, it's less well known, but nevertheless a fantastic wrapping bread just waiting for a healthy filling – chicken shawarma, anyone?

PITTA BREAD

So easy to make, you could even bake these pitta breads with your fillings prepared and ready to go inside for a super-quick lunch. Beautifully fresh, they will bring the Levant to your kitchen.

MAKES 10 PITTA BREADS

7g fast-action/easy-bake dried yeast

2 tbsp extra virgin olive oil

500g strong white flour

8g natural fine sea salt

You will need:

baking stone or an upturned baking tray

wooden peel, or baking sheet scattered with
semolina/polenta

1

Put your mixing bowl on the scales and set it to 0g, then measure the yeast. Set the scale back to 0g before measuring the next ingredient. Add 280g/280ml lukewarm water to the bowl. (You need a quick fermentation to help the bread puff up.) Add the oil.

2

Set the scale back to 0g, then add the flour. Put the bowl to one side and weigh the salt separately in a small bowl on the scales. (This makes it easier to correct in case you add too much on top of the other ingredients.) Add to the bowl with the flour, then add the oil.

3

Using only one hand and a circular movement, bring together the ingredients to form a dough. It will feel quite firm. Put the dough on the table and, using your mixing hand, stretch it and fold it, or roll it back onto itself. Repeat the process, rotating the dough regularly to make sure that all the dough has been thoroughly kneaded. You should be done within 6 minutes of starting to stretch, fold and stretch again. This dough will be no trouble at all, as it is quite firm, allowing the steam produced during baking to separate it easily, thereby creating the pocket in its centre.

4

Forty-five minutes before baking, put a baking stone or upturned baking tray into the oven and preheat the oven to 240°C (220°C fan oven) Gas 9, or as high as your oven can go. Your baking stone, or upturned baking tray, needs to be very hot. Cover the dough with a shower cap or plastic bag and leave in a warm place to prove for 30 minutes or until roughly doubled in size.

5

Divide the dough into ten 80g pieces. Shape them into rounds, then, with the palm of your hand, rock them back and forth on the work surface until they look more oval. Cover them with the mixing bowl and bench-rest for 5 minutes.

6

Start flattening the dough rounds with your rolling pin by placing it in the middle of each piece and then rolling up and down a few times, flip them over a couple of times during the rolling process. Make sure that they are even, about 3mm thick, throughout, with no fat lip on either end.

Put two or three pittas on the wooden peel, or prepared baking sheet, and deposit them carefully on the baking stone or upturned baking tray. Cook for just 3 minutes. You don't need to turn them over. You do not want any colour on them. Just watch them gradually puffing up in quite a dramatic fashion. Take them out and wrap them immediately in a damp tea towel to keep them soft. You will almost certainly put them back in the oven before filling them when you are ready to use them.

TIP

You can freeze some of your pittas to eat later. They defrost very quickly – you could even put them straight into your toaster for immediate action!

LAVASH

This flatbread is associated with Armenian baking, but you can find versions of lavash from Turkey, Kurdistan, Syria and Lebanon – right up through Central Asia. It's a fantastic bread to wrap around spice-and-herb-infused shredded, grilled meat or homemade deep-fried falafel.

MAKES 10 LAVASH

7g fast-action/easy-bake dried yeast

2 tbsp of extra virgin olive oil

450g strong white flour, plus extra for dusting

6g natural fine sea salt

2 tsp seeds (nigella, sesame, or poppy seeds),
whole cumin or za'atar

You will need:

baking stone or an upturned baking tray

wooden peel, or baking sheet scattered with
semolina/polenta

1

Put your mixing bowl on the scales and set it to 0g, then measure
the yeast. Set the scale back to 0g before measuring the next
ingredient. Add 280g/280ml water to the bowl. (Adjust the
temperature of the water according to your kitchen
environment.) Add the oil.

Set the scale back to 0g, then add the flour. Put the bowl to one side and weigh the salt separately in a small bowl on the scales. (This makes it easier to correct in case you add too much on top of the other ingredients.) Add to the bowl with the flour, then add the oil.

3

Using only one hand, mix the ingredients together until they form a loose dough. Put the dough on an unfloured work surface and, using the heel of your mixing hand, start to knead it by stretching, folding and stretching it again.

4

When the dough has begun to look better combined and smoother, gather it together with the scraper and add the seeds to the centre of the dough. Fold one end of the dough over the seeds so that they are trapped in the dough and then perform the same kneading action for just long enough for the dough to be evenly speckled with the seeds.

5

Cover the dough with a shower cap or plastic bag and leave in a warm place to prove for 30 minutes or until roughly doubled in size. Divide it into ten 80g pieces. Shape these into rounds, then cover them with the mixing bowl and bench-rest for 5 minutes.

6

Forty-five minutes before baking, put a baking stone or upturned baking tray into the oven and preheat the oven to 240°C (220°C fan oven) Gas 9, or as high as your oven can go. Your baking stone, or upturned baking tray, needs to be very hot.

7

Put one piece of dough on a well-floured work surface. Flour the top of the lavash well and start rolling from the centre up and down, making sure that you rotate the dough 90° each time to retain a circular shape. Flip each circle over a couple of times while rolling. They should be very thin indeed, almost to the extent that you can see the work surface underneath.

8

Put the flattened lavash on the wooden peel, or prepared baking sheet, and deposit it carefully onto the baking stone. It will bake very quickly: cook for 30 seconds then turn and cook for another 30 seconds. It will be covered with blisters, like bubbles, almost immediately. Don't allow the lavash to take on any colour – a few golden spots here and there is fine, but any more than that and you won't have a wrapping bread, but something more like a wafer-thin cracker, or a poppadum. Put the lavash in a damp tea towel to keep them nice and pliable until ready to serve.

TIP

You can freeze some of your lavash to eat later. These are very handy for a quick, healthy snack. Just put your hot filling in the centre and wrap the lavash around it. Put it under a preheated grill (or in a panini press, if you have one), and heat through until some of the lavash starts getting some colour on those bubbles that appeared when first baked.

Daily Bread

Here is a selection of three breads that could be your daily staples – loaves for everyday enjoyment. From a mighty white to a healthy Granary and wholemeal loaves, they offer a variety of flavours and address some dietary concerns. Make them time and time again until they come naturally to you, then move on to other recipes. Never feel restricted that these are the only recipes for you to follow. Just use them to practise your breadmaking skills, and then, when you're proficient, follow your own path.

All three recipes are based on a poolish method. A poolish is a half-and-half mix of flour and water with a bit of yeast. This bit of dough that ferments in advance, well ahead of any kneading, is also called a 'preferment'. This method gives you a lot of flexibility, as the initial mixture can be made up to two days ahead of making the dough. This improves the flavour and also allows you to substantially reduce the amount of yeast used in the final loaf, which gives a more natural and gentle fermentation.

WHITE LOAF

A homemade white loaf is tasty and satisfying, and a far cry from most bought loaves. Nutritionally speaking, however, white bread is not perfect, because the bran and wheatgerm are all removed, and with them most of the trace minerals, good natural fats, folic acid, and so on. To bring some goodness back into the loaf I have added a little wholemeal flour to this recipe.

In modern white bread flour, the gluten ratio can be very high, as seen in Canadian wheat, which has a staggering 18 per cent gluten. That excess gluten will give much more volume to the loaf but, on the other hand, it doesn't make the bread easy on your stomach during digestion, especially if a lot of yeast, white sugar, additives and improvers are also used, as in supermarket breads. You should be aware of all this, but don't be deterred from making a good, honest white loaf because, if it's made properly and with a longer fermentation, a good white loaf can be a delicious indulgence. Start preparations the day before.

For the poolish (preferment):

1g fast-action/easy-bake dried yeast

50g strong white flour

For the final dough:

3g fast-action/easy-bake dried yeast)

420g strong white flour, plus extra for dusting

30g rye or any wholemeal flour

8g fine natural salt

oil, for greasing (if using a loaf tin)

You will need:

proving basket or a mixing bowl lined with a tea towel,
or a 900g loaf tin

baking stone or an upturned baking tray

wooden peel, or baking sheet scattered with semolina/polenta

razor blade

1

Start preparations the day before. To make the poolish, put a bowl on the scales and set it to 0g, then measure the yeast. Set the scale back to 0g before measuring the next ingredient. Add the flour and 50g/50ml water. Mix thoroughly together and leave in a warm place for 1 hour, just long enough to get the fermentation started. Cover and put in the fridge for 8–48 hours (this is a very flexible and easy-going poolish). This will enhance the flavour of your loaf and allow you to reduce the amount of yeast considerably when you come to make your final dough.

2

The next day, put your mixing bowl on the scales and set it to 0g, then measure the yeast. Set the scale back to 0g before measuring the next ingredient. Add 275g/275ml water to the bowl. (Adjust the temperature of the water according to your kitchen environment.)

3

Set the scale back to 0g, then add the flours. Put the bowl to one side and weigh the salt separately in a small bowl on the scales. (This makes it easier to correct in case you add too much on top of the other ingredients.) Add to the bowl with the flour.

4

Add the poolish to the mixing bowl, making sure that you scrape as much as possible of the poolish into your final dough.

5

Using only one hand in a circular movement, bring together the ingredients to form a dough. Put the dough on the work surface and, using the heel of your mixing hand, stretch the dough and fold it, or roll it back onto itself, then repeat the process, rotating the dough regularly to ensure that all the dough has been thoroughly kneaded. This should take 6–8 minutes at most; any longer than that would not benefit the gluten development or the volume of your loaf.

6

Scrape together all your dough to create a ball, then put it back into the bowl, cover it with a shower cap or plastic bag and leave it in a warm place to prove for the first rise for 1½ hours or until it has roughly doubled in size. (If you wish, you can knock back the dough after 45 minutes to regenerate the fermentation to add to the structure of your loaf, then leave it in a warm place to prove for another 45 minutes to make the 1½ hours in total.)

7

Use a scraper to help you remove the dough from the bowl and onto a lightly floured work surface. Be careful not to use too much extra flour; it is better to use the stickiness of the dough to your advantage. Pre-shape your dough into a round (or a rough oval shape, if you will be using a loaf tin), cover it again with something plastic, then bench-rest for 10 minutes.

To make a round loaf

1

With both hands slightly curved, squeeze the base of your dough, pressing together the two sides of the dough tightly, then repeat the same movement while rotating the dough. The loaf will become taller and tighter on the outside. Repeat this process four or five times Repeat this process just to create tension all over the loaf. Complete the sealing of your loaf by placing your hands on both sides of the dough and rotating it quickly four or five times in a row on the same spot. Immediately put it upside down – seam up. (The seam should be tightly sealed with no gaping hole. If it's too large, this would be as a result of having added too much flour during shaping.)

2

Put the loaf in a proving basket or a mixing bowl lined with a tea towel, then prove the loaf for the second rise for 1–1½ hours or until the dough is at least level with the rim of the proving basket, perhaps even doming over it, nice and round. Meanwhile, put a baking stone or upturned baking tray into the oven and preheat the oven to 240°C (220°C fan oven) Gas 9.

3

Turn the loaf over carefully onto the wooden peel, or prepared baking sheet, cushioning its fall with your hand so that it doesn't deflate. With the corner of a razor blade held at a 45-degree angle, slash the top of your bread in a hashtag-like pattern about 2mm deep, tilting the blade.

4

Put the loaf on the baking stone or upturned baking tray. Spray the sides of the oven chamber to create steam and bake for 25 minutes, then rotate the loaf and give it another 10–15 minutes until golden brown and when you tap on the base it sounds hollow (a darker colour will give a more interesting flavour). Take the loaf out of the oven and cool it on a wire rack.

To use a loaf tin

1

Grease a 900g loaf tin. Turn the oval pre-shaped dough upside down (seam up) and smooth-side down against the work surface. Flatten it gently, then fold the left and right sides so that they meet in the middle, then press them down firmly. Now fold the dough towards you once and again, using your fingertips or the heel of your hand each time to seal it. Turn the dough over (with the seam down), and now place both hands in the middle of your loaf and extend it evenly and gently outwards, until it is the right length for the tin. Make sure that the seam is facing down as you lower it into the tin.

2

Cover the loaf with a shower cap or plastic bag again and leave it in a warm place to prove for the second rise of 1–1½ hours until the dough has risen above the top of the tin – nice and healthily plump (although not over the sides, because then it would have over-proved). Meanwhile, put an upturned baking tray into the oven and preheat the oven to 240°C (220°C fan oven) Gas 9.

3

Flour the top of the loaf with white flour, if you like. Using the corner of a razor blade held at a 45-degree angle to the loaf, slash the top of the loaf in a straight line about 1cm deep.

4

Put your tin on the upturned baking tray. Spray the sides of the oven chamber to create steam and bake for 25 minutes, then rotate the tin and give it another 10 minutes until golden brown and when you tap on the base it sounds hollow. Take the loaf out of the oven and turn it out of the tin onto a wire rack to cool.

GRANARY TIN

This loaf has a definite caramelised taste as a result of the malted wheat flakes in the Granary flour and the addition of flavoured sugars to the mixture. This is a great bread for sandwiches, but really it is a true all-rounder. And there is nothing to stop you from making a round loaf or a bloomer. Start preparations the day before.

For the poolish (preferment):

1g fast-action/easy-bake dried yeast

50g strong white flour

For the final dough:

3g fast-action/easy-bake dried yeast

225g strong white flour, plus extra for dusting

225g malted Granary flour

8g natural fine sea salt

1 tsp of black treacle or barley syrup (optional, see Tip)

oil, for greasing

You will need:

baking tray

900g loaf tin, or a round proving basket or a mixing bowl
lined with a tea towel

baking stone or an upturned baking tray

1

Start preparations the day before. To make the poolish, put a bowl on the scales and set it to 0g, then measure the yeast. Set the scale back to 0g before measuring the next ingredient. Add the flour and 50g/50ml water. Mix thoroughly together and leave in a warm place for 1 hour, just long enough to get the fermentation started. Cover and put in the fridge for 8–48 hours. This will enhance the flavour of your loaf and allow you to reduce the amount of yeast considerably when you come to make your final dough.

2

The next day, put your mixing bowl on the scales and set it to 0g, then measure the yeast. Set the scale back to 0g before measuring the next ingredient. Add 290g/290ml water to the bowl. (Adjust the temperature of the water according to your kitchen environment.)

3

Set the scale back to 0g, then add the flour. Put the bowl to one side and weigh the salt separately in a small bowl on the scales. (This makes it easier to correct in case you add too much on top of the other ingredients.) Add to the bowl with the flour and add the black treacle, if using.

4

Add the poolish to the mixing bowl, making sure that you scrape as much as possible of the poolish into your final dough.

5

Using only one hand in a circular movement, bring together the ingredients to form a dough. Place the dough on your work surface and, using the heel of your mixing hand, stretch the dough and fold it, or roll it back onto itself, then repeat the process, rotating the dough regularly to ensure that all the dough has been thoroughly kneaded. This should take 6–8 minutes at most; any longer than that would not benefit the gluten development or the volume of your loaf.

6

Scrape together all your dough to create a ball, then put it back into the bowl, cover it with a shower cap or plastic bag and leave it in a warm place to prove for the first rise for 1½ hours or until has roughly doubled in size. (If you wish, you can knock back the dough after 45 minutes to regenerate the fermentation to add to the structure of your loaf, then leave it in a warm place for another 45 minutes to make the 1½ hours in total.)

7

Use a scraper to get the dough out of the bowl and onto a lightly floured work surface. Be careful not to use too much extra flour; it is better to use the stickiness of the dough to your advantage. Pre-shape the loaf into an oval, cover with plastic again, or a bowl, then bench-rest for 10 minutes.

8

Grease a 900g loaf tin. Turn the oval-shaped loaf upside down (seam up) and smooth-side down against the work surface. Flatten it gently, then fold the left and right sides so that they meet in the middle and press them down firmly. Now fold the dough towards you once again, using your fingertips or the heel of your hand each time to seal it. Turn the dough over (with the seam down), and now place both hands in the middle of your loaf and extend it evenly and gently outwards, until it is the right length for the tin. Make sure that the seam is facing down as you lower it into the tin.

9

Leave the loaf in a warm place to prove for the second rise of 1–1½ hours until the dough has risen above the top of the tin – nice and healthily plump (although not over the sides, because then it would have over-proved). Meanwhile, put a baking stone or an upturned baking tray into the oven and preheat the oven to 230°C (210°C fan oven) Gas 8.

10

Flour the top of loaf with white flour, if you like. Using the corner of a razor blade held at a right angle, slash the top of the loaf in a straight line about 1cm deep.

11

Put your tin on the upturned baking tray. Spray the sides of the oven chamber to create steam. Bake the loaf for 25 minutes, then rotate the tin and give it another 10 minutes until golden brown and when you tap on the base it sounds hollow. Take the loaf out of the oven and turn it out of the tin onto a wire rack to cool.

TIP

You can skip the black treacle if you wish; it is just adding a pleasant caramelised taste to the crust.

WHOLEMEAL LOAF

This is the very healthy option in your daily bread selection. I'm always a bit wary of a 100 per cent wholemeal loaf because I find them pretty dense, and we all like a bit of lightness in life. Here I have incorporated some white flour for that very reason (making it more like a brown bread). Start preparations the day before.

For the poolish (preferment):

1g fast-action/easy-bake dried yeast

50g strong white flour

For the final dough:

5g yeast

225g strong wholemeal flour, plus extra for dusting

225g strong white flour, plus extra for dusting

8g natural fine sea salt

1 tsp black treacle or barley syrup (optional, see Tip page 116)

You will need:

baking tray

round proving basket or a mixing bowl lined with a tea towel

baking stone or an upturned baking tray

wooden peel, or baking sheet scattered with
semolina/polenta

1

Start preparations the day before. To make the poolish, put a bowl on the scales and set it to 0g, then measure the yeast. Set the scale back to 0g before measuring the next ingredient. Add the flour and 50g/50ml water. Mix thoroughly together and leave in a warm place for 1 hour, just long enough to get the fermentation started. Cover and put in the fridge for 8–48 hours. (This will enhance the flavour of your loaf and allow you to reduce the amount of yeast considerably when you come to make your final dough.)

2

The next day, put your mixing bowl on the scales and set it to 0g, then measure the yeast. Set the scale back to 0g before measuring the next ingredient. Add 300g/300ml water to the bowl. (Adjust the temperature of the water according to your kitchen environment.)

3

Set the scale back to 0g, then add the flours. Put the bowl to one side and weigh the salt separately in a small bowl on the scales. (This makes it easier to correct in case you add too much on top of the other ingredients.) Add to the bowl with the flour, then add the black treacle, if using.

4

Add the poolish to the mixing bowl, making sure that you scrape as much as possible of the poolish into your final dough.

5

Using only one hand in a circular movement, bring together the ingredients to form a dough. Put the dough on your work surface and, using the heel of your mixing hand, stretch the dough and fold it, or roll it back onto itself, then repeat the process, rotating the dough regularly to make sure that all the dough has been thoroughly kneaded. This should take 6–8 minutes at most; any longer than that would not benefit the gluten development or the volume of your loaf.

6

Scrape together all your dough to create a ball, then put it back into the bowl, cover it with a shower cap or plastic bag and leave it in a warm place to prove for the first rise for 1½ hours or until it has roughly doubled in size. (If you wish, you can knock back the dough after 45 minutes to regenerate the fermentation to add to the structure of your loaf, then leave it in a warm place to prove for another 45 minutes to make the 1½ hours in total.)

7

Use a scraper to help you remove the dough from the bowl and onto a lightly floured work surface. Be careful not to add too much extra flour; it is better to use the stickiness of the dough to your advantage. Shape your dough into a round, then bench-rest for 10 minutes.

8

Now start shaping your loaf. With both hands slightly curved, squeeze the base of your dough, pressing together the two sides of the dough tightly, then repeat the same movement while rotating the dough. The loaf will become taller and tighter on the outside. Repeat this process four or five times to create tension all over the loaf. Complete the sealing of your loaf by placing your hands on both sides of the dough and rotating it quickly four or five times in a row on the same spot. Immediately put it upside down – seam up. (The seam should be tightly sealed with no gaping hole. If it's too large, this would be as a result of having added too much flour during shaping.)

9

Put the loaf in a proving basket or a mixing bowl lined with a tea towel, then leave it in a warm place to prove for the second rise for 1–1½ hours or until the dough has risen at least level with the rim of the proving basket, perhaps even doming over it, nice and round. Meanwhile, put a baking stone or upturned baking tray into the oven and preheat the oven to 240°C (220°C fan oven) Gas 9.

10

Turn the loaf over carefully onto the wooden peel, or prepared baking sheet, cushioning its fall with your hand so that it doesn't deflate. With a corner of a razor blade held at a 45-degree angle, slash the top of the loaf in a hashtag-like pattern about 2mm deep.

Put the loaf on the baking stone or an upturned baking tray. Spray the sides of the oven chamber to create steam and bake the loaf for 25 minutes, then rotate the loaf and give it another 10 minutes, until golden brown. Take the loaf out of the oven and cool on a cooling rack.

Variation

You can make your own version of this loaf using 100 per cent wholemeal flour. In which case you will have to increase the water to 350g/350ml, because the bran in your wholemeal flour will naturally absorb a lot of liquid.

Enriched Doughs

The morning treats in this section are a classic brioche, cinnamon scrolls and a versatile bun dough that you can turn into breakfast rolls, burger buns, hot-dog buns or a sweetish sandwich tin loaf. An 'enriched' dough simply means that you're adding another ingredient, or perhaps you have added a few additional ingredients to the basic bread dough comprising flour, water, yeast and salt. Any addition of fruits, seeds, meat, cheese or vegetables would also be considered an enrichment.

CLASSIC BRIOCHE

Although this might go against my principles of exclusively using my hands for breadmaking, for the brioche I would rather use an electric stand mixer. The butter needs to be incorporated as quickly as possible to avoid melting it, which would make your brioche very greasy, thereby ruining it.

A good brioche is an overnight affair: you make the dough the day before and give it a nice long, cold fermentation in the fridge so that it slowly develops great flavours and a slight acidity that makes eating your own brioche such a memorable experience.

8g fast-action/easy-bake dried yeast

6 medium eggs, beaten, plus 1 beaten egg, to glaze

35g/35ml full-fat or semi-skimmed milk,
at room temperature

30g sugar

500g strong white flour, plus extra for dusting

14g natural fine sea salt

300g unsalted butter, softened

oil, for greasing

You will need:

electric stand mixer

2   900g loaf tins

1

Put your mixing bowl on the scales and set it to 0g, then measure
the yeast. Set the scale back to 0g before measuring each
ingredient. Add the 6 eggs, the milk, sugar and flour.

2

Put the bowl to one side and weigh the salt separately in a small bowl on the scales. (This makes it easier to correct in case you add too much on top of the other ingredients.) Add to the bowl with the flour mixture.

3

Use a dough hook of an electric stand mixer to knead the mixture for 6 minutes at medium speed followed by 4 minutes at high speed (you're trying to stretch that gluten to the maximum to get a lovely teary crumb later when your brioche is baked). Stop the mixer and give the dough a rest for 5 minutes.

4

In the meantime, divide the softened butter into quarters. With the mixer running at top speed, add a quarter of the butter. When the butter has disappeared into the dough, continue in the same way with the remaining butter, a quarter at a time. When all the butter has been incorporated (the dough should have left the side of the mixing bowl to wrap itself around the hook), stop the mixer and use your hands to shape the dough into a ball.

5

Put the dough back in the bowl, cover with a shower cap or plastic bag and leave in a warm place for 2–3 hours until it has doubled in size. Put the dough onto a lightly floured work surface and knock it back by bringing each side into the middle then turning it over. Put the dough back into the bowl, cover it again as before and put it in the fridge for 12–18 hours (this is loosely called 'overnight' in baking books).

6

The next day, take the dough out of the fridge and put it onto a lightly floured work surface. Sprinkle a little more flour on top and work the dough gently, just to soften the butter, which will have hardened during that long stay in the fridge.

7

Divide the dough into 12 pieces of 100g each and shape them into rounds. Cover the dough and bench-rest for 10 minutes, but if your kitchen is really warm, especially in the summer, begin to shape your loaves straight away rather than running the risk of the butter melting.

8

Line two 900g loaf tins with baking paper. Shape the pieces of dough tightly into bun shapes. Place the buns in a staggered pattern in the prepared loaf tins. Cover them loosely with lightly oiled plastic wrap and leave them in a warm place to prove for 2 hours. The brioche should rise well above the rim of the tin. Meanwhile, preheat the oven to 200°C (180°C fan oven) Gas 6.

9

Brush the brioche with the beaten egg for glazing. Spray the sides of the oven chamber to create steam and bake for 25 minutes or until golden brown. Leave the brioches to cool in the tins for 10 minutes before carefully turning onto a wire rack to cool. When pulled apart, the crumb should be very light and easy to tear.

CINNAMON SCROLLS

These scrolls are a real treat with their traditional filling of a scrumptious cinnamon, sugar and butter spread. Scandinavian baking is not shy when it comes to mixing flavours to achieve a fabulous taste, with the addition of spices, seeds, flavoursome sugars or citrus zest. Here cardamom and cinnamon meet dark muscovado sugar and butter to become those very sticky, buttery indulgent buns.

8g fast-action/easy-bake dried yeast

300g/300ml full-fat or semi-skimmed milk,
at room temperature

500g strong white flour, plus extra for dusting

2 tsp ground cardamom (it is best is to use whole cardamom
ground in a pestle and mortar – discard the husks and grind
the seeds until fine)

8g natural fine sea salt

40g caster sugar

50g unsalted butter, softened

For the cinnamon filling:

200g unsalted butter, softened

200g dark muscovado sugar

30g ground cinnamon

For the glaze:

200g caster sugar

1 cinnamon stick

zest and juice of 1 orange

zest and juice of 1 lemon

1 bay leaf

3 cloves

You will need:

small baking sheet

1

Put your mixing bowl on the scales and set it to 0g, then measure the yeast. Set the scale back to 0g before measuring the next ingredient. Add the milk to the bowl.

2

Set the scale back to 0g, then add the flour and ground cardamom. Put the bowl to one side and weigh the salt separately in a small bowl on the scales. (This makes it easier to correct in case you add too much on top of the other ingredients.) Add to the bowl with the flour, and add the sugar and butter.

3

Using only one hand in a circular movement, bring together the ingredients to form a dough. Put the dough on your work surface and, using the heel of your mixing hand, stretch it and fold it, or roll it back onto itself, then repeat the process, rotating the dough regularly to ensure that all the dough has been thoroughly kneaded. This should take 6–8 minutes; any longer than that would not benefit the gluten development or the volume of your loaf.

4

Scrape together all your dough to create a ball, then put it back into the bowl, cover it with a shower cap or plastic bag and leave it in a warm place to prove for 1 hour or until it has roughly doubled in size (the sugar will speed up the fermentation, making the proving times for both the first and second rises considerably shorter).

5

To prepare the cinnamon filling, put the softened butter in a bowl and add the sugar and cinnamon. Be aware that if you make the filling well ahead of time and put it in the fridge, the butter will harden again making it impossible to spread. You will then need to allow it to soften before using it, or simply keep it out of the fridge. When you are ready to use it, cream it again, to ensure that it is smooth.

6

Take the dough out of the bowl and put it on a floured work surface. (Exercise restraint with the flour; you can always add more as you go along.) Put the rolling pin in the middle of the dough and start rolling it up and down until you have a length of 40cm. Rotate the dough and roll it out as before, until you have a roughly 40cm square. Press down on the nearside of the square to create a flat lip that you will brush with water to help you seal the scroll later on.

7

Line a small baking sheet with baking paper. Make sure that your cinnamon butter is nice and soft and creamy, then spread it evenly over the dough except for the lip that you flattened across the side nearest to you. Try to spread the butter right up to the edges.

8

Start rolling the buttered dough towards you, keeping it as tight as possible, like a Swiss roll shape. Seal the dough by moistening the flat lip with water and then pressing it against the roll. Cut the roll into 12 even slices. (I usually cut the dough into four equal quarters, then I cut each quarter into three.) Lay the individual scrolls neatly flat on the prepared baking sheet, leaving just enough space between the scrolls to allow them to prove.

9

Cover the tray loosely with plastic wrap or put it in a large plastic bag and leave the scrolls in a warm place to prove for their second rise for 30 minutes or until the scrolls are touching each other, making them look like little plump squares. Meanwhile, Preheat the oven to 200°C (180°C fan oven) Gas 6.

Spray the sides of the oven chamber to create steam. Bake the scrolls for 15 minutes or until dark brown on top.

11

While the scrolls are baking, put the glaze ingredients in a heavy-based saucepan over a medium heat. Bring the mixture to the boil, then reduce the heat and simmer for 5 minutes. Remove the pan from the heat.

12

As soon as the scrolls come out of the oven, brush them generously with the sugar glaze. Slide them very carefully from the tray onto a wire rack to cool. (Don't leave them to cool in the tray because it will become a hammer-and-chisel job to get them out when cold!) Eat them warm with a cup of tea or coffee – ideally after a long walk in order to deserve all the calories you're about to consume.

Variations

You could use the brioche dough on page 125 for this recipe, and how indulgent and decadent those buns would be! If you have already made a number of different doughs, start thinking about how you could tweak this recipe. You could take them beyond their original intention and use them for something else, listening to your inspiration. Vive la création!

You could swap the filling above for a chocolate or nut filling (praline) or a flavoured pastry cream (vanilla, chocolate or caramel), if you like.

BUN DOUGH

This is a generic enriched and very versatile dough that could also be used for any recipe that calls for a slightly sweet-tasting crumb, such as a burger roll, a lobster roll, a hot-dog roll, Devonshire splits (small buns filled with jam and cream), muffins or a *pain de mie* sandwich loaf. You could even use it for a simplified scrolls dough (see page 129). Here, I will show you how to make some seeded buns using this recipe.

MAKES 12 BUNS

8g fast-action/easy-bake dried yeast

300g/300ml full-fat or semi-skimmed milk,
at room temperature

225g strong white flour, plus extra for dusting

225g plain white flour

7g natural fine sea salt

15g caster sugar

50g unsalted butter, softened

1 egg, beaten, to glaze

seeds (sesame, poppy, pumpkin, sunflower, nigella,
linseed or chia), to sprinkle

You will need:

baking sheet

1

Put your mixing bowl on the scales and set it to 0g, then measure the yeast. Set the scale back to 0g before measuring the next ingredient. Add the milk to the bowl.

2

Set the scale back to 0g, then add the flours. Put the bowl to one side and weigh the salt separately in a small bowl on the scales. (This makes it easier to correct in case you add too much on top of the other ingredients.) Add to the bowl with the flour and add the sugar and butter.

3

Using only one hand in a circular movement, bring the ingredients together to form a dough. It will feel quite firm. Put the dough on your work surface and, using the heel of your mixing hand, stretch it and fold it, or roll it back onto itself, then keep repeating the process, rotating the dough regularly to ensure that all the dough has been thoroughly kneaded. This should take 6–8 minutes; anything more than that would not benefit the gluten development or the volume.

4

Scrape together all your dough to create a ball, then put it back into the bowl, cover with a shower cap or plastic bag and leave it in a warm place to prove for 1 hour. (Because there is sugar and also a fair amount of yeast in the recipe, fermentation will be quite fast for both the first and second rises).

5

Put the dough on a lightly floured work surface and divide it into 12 pieces of around 70g each. (If you want something larger, like a bap, divide into nine pieces instead.) They do not need a bench-rest, so you can shape them into buns straight away. Cup the palm of your hand over a piece of dough and rotate it quickly on the same spot about six times until the bun becomes taller, smoother and is firm to the touch. Repeat with the remaining dough pieces.

6

Put the buns well spaced on a baking sheet so that they don't merge into one another while proving. Brush the buns with the beaten egg and sprinkle them with your chosen seeds. Cover them loosely with plastic wrap or put the baking sheet in a large plastic bag and leave them in a warm place to prove for 40 minutes or until they have doubled in size. (It is important not to leave them to prove for too long because that might result in them turning out flat.) Meanwhile, preheat the oven to 200°C (180°C fan oven) Gas 6.

7

Spray the sides of the oven chamber to create steam. Bake the buns for 12 minutes or until golden. Cool on a wire rack. They will be soft after they cool down and absolutely perfect for sandwiches.

Pastry Crusts

For those times when you feel like baking something that is less strenuous than bread, here are three classic foundation pastry doughs that will equip you to deal with a large selection of sweet and savoury recipes. I have also added a recipe for wheat crackers that are a great hit with everybody and very simple to make.

PUFF PASTRY

When you open a baking book at the puff pastry or croissant section, it might seem that you need a PhD in structural engineering to understand the process behind it, but things are actually a lot simpler than they appear. I will demystify the process for you, so that in the end you will wonder what all the fuss was about.

First, we need to make the base, then proceed to the lamination, or layering, of the dough. I like to use French unsalted butter for lamination because it is drier than English or Irish butter, which is lovely but too creamy for this particular task. A drier butter will remain firmer when spread and it is less likely to ooze out of the dough.

When you have mastered the process you will be able to make many great pastries, such as cheese straws, tarte tatin, vol-au-vents, mille-feuilles, sausage rolls and pies of all kinds.

MAKES TWO 500G BLOCKS

For the base:

500g strong white flour, plus extra for dusting

12g natural fine sea salt

80g unsalted butter, ideally French, cut into small pieces

10g/10ml white wine vinegar or lemon juice

For the lamination:

420g unsalted butter, French ideally

1

Weigh the flour and salt separately, then sieve them together into a mixing bowl. Rub the butter into the flour using your fingertips.

2

Make a well in the middle and pour in 230g/230ml ice-cold water and the vinegar. (The white wine vinegar will make the gluten stretchier and prevent the pastry from discolouring. When puff pastry is stored in the fridge for a while it can develop little black spots on the surface, giving it an unattractive greyish appearance.)

3

Using only one hand, bring the ingredients together into a rough dough, ensuring that all the ingredients are fully combined. That will be all the kneading that is required – to be precise, no kneading. If the gluten is developed too much, when you come to laminating, it will be much harder to roll. Wrap the dough tightly in plastic wrap or a wax wrap and leave it to rest for at least 3 hours in the fridge. (Even better would be to make the dough the day or the evening before.)

4

Put the chilled dough on a generously floured work surface. Using your fists, turn your base into a 25cm square and, using a rolling pin, create flaps around that base so that you have a thick centre and four flaps about 5–6mm thick, one on each side (they should be thinner than the centre of the base but they shouldn't be wafer thin).

5

Tap the butter for the lamination with the rolling pin, then sprinkle a little flour on top to prevent the butter from sticking to the rolling pin. It is important that the texture and softness of the butter matches that of the dough; if the butter is too hard, it is likely that it will go through the layers of the dough and ruin your lamination. If the butter is too soft, it will melt and ooze out of the dough, spreading everywhere except inside the dough.

6

Put the butter on the raised centre of dough. Take the bottom flap, and fold it completely over the butter, so that you can't see any butter, and seal it firmly. Take the top flap and cover 80 per cent of the first flap, then do the same with the flaps on the left and the right sides, bringing them into the middle, or slightly overlapping each other, creating a line running away from you, the seam. This secures the butter inside, preventing the rolling pin from pushing it away when you extend the base in the next step.

7

To extend the base, hold the rolling pin firmly at each end and start pressing gently forward, four or five times, along the base, spreading the butter. Your base will have a succession of ridges on its surface. You are going to roll out those ridges one after the other to smooth them out until you end up with a flat, thick base.

8

Put the rolling pin in the middle of the base and start rolling away from you with controlled pressure. (Be aware that we tend to press too hard when laminating, which can tear the dough, revealing the butter inside.) Roll gently back towards you until the rolling pin is back in the middle, then, using the same amount of force as when you were rolling away from yourself, continue rolling towards the bottom of the base. You can also flip the dough over from time to time to create an even extension by ensuring that both sides of the dough are being flattened against the work surface. You will need to flour your work surface at regular intervals to prevent the dough from sticking to it, as this could also ruin the layering of your puff pastry.

9

Repeat this up-and-down motion until you have extended the base to 80cm in length. When you have done that, brush the excess flour off your dough using a pastry brush on both sides, then fold in thirds from the top or bottom. You have just achieved your first single fold, or 'turn' as it is sometimes called.

10

Rotate your dough by a quarter of a turn. Imagine that your puff pastry is a book, and turn it towards you so that the 'spine' of your book is on the left with the 'pages' (the seam) on the opposite side. You will return to this position during the entire lamination process when you come to extend the dough again.

11

Now repeat exactly the same action as at the beginning. With the rolling pin held firmly at both ends, start gently pressing forward four or five times, moving along the base. You will have created a succession of ridges on the surface and you're going to roll out those ridges, one after the other, to smooth them out and end up with a flat, although still thick, base. Place the rolling pin in the middle of the base and start going up and down the dough firmly, but without excessive pressure. Once again, flip the dough over from time to time to keep it even. Don't forget to flour your work surface at regular intervals to prevent the dough from sticking to it.

12

Extend the dough to 80cm, then brush off the excess flour all over, using a pastry brush. Now fold it in three. You have now finished your second single fold (or turn). (These two single folds are also described as a double fold, or double turn.) Using a single finger, make two small indents to remind you how far along you are with the lamination. It is imperative that you give the puff pastry a rest, wrapped in plastic wrap or a wax wrap, in the fridge for 45–60 minutes. You wouldn't be able to carry on with more folds straight away in any case because your dough would not stretch easily at all. If you're leaving it in the fridge for much more than 1 hour, take it out for 15 minutes so that the butter can soften a little bit before more rolling-pin action (the butter will always harden more than the dough).

13

Take your puff pastry out of the fridge, and put the 'spine' on the left as before. Then give it, as described above, a second double fold. Return the pastry to the fridge wrapped in plastic wrap or a wax wrap, and rest it for another 45–60 minutes.

14

Take the puff pastry out of the fridge again and complete the last double fold, starting with the 'spine' on the left as before. By now you will have completed three double folds (six single folds), since beginning your lamination.

15

Lamination is now complete. Cut the dough into two equal pieces and wrap individually in plastic wrap or a wax wrap, then leave the dough to rest for at least 3 hours in the fridge before using it in your recipe. Use the dough within 4 days. Puff pastry freezes exceptionally well. Just defrost it in the fridge the day before you need it.

SUGAR PASTRY

This crust can be used as a base for any sweet tarts: fruit pies, fruit tartlets, Bakewell tarts or any other sweet flans.

MAKES TWO 400G BLOCKS

400g plain flour, plus extra for dusting

a pinch of salt

250g caster sugar

100g unsalted butter, cut into small pieces

2 eggs, beaten

1

Weigh the flour, salt and sugar separately, then sieve them together into a mixing bowl.

2

Rub in the butter using your fingertips until it resembles fine breadcrumbs. Make a well in the centre of the mixture and stir in the eggs to make a dough. (When making any pastry crusts, it is very important not to over-work the dough, as that will make the crust too tough.) Mix the dough lightly in the bowl, then take it out and work it quickly on a lightly floured work surface to make it more homogenous.

<u>3</u>

Cut the dough into two equal pieces and wrap individually in plastic wrap or a wax wrap, then leave the dough to rest for at least 3 hours in the fridge before using it in your recipe. (Making the dough the day before would be even better.) Use the dough within 5 days. Sugar pastry freezes very well. Just defrost it in the fridge the day before you need it.

SHORTCRUST PASTRY

This crust is perfect for savoury flans, Cornish pasties and meat or vegetable pies.

300g plain flour, plus extra for dusting

a pinch of salt

150g cold unsalted butter, cut into small pieces

50g/50ml full-fat or semi-skimmed milk, cold

1

Weigh the flour and salt separately, then sieve them together into a mixing bowl. Rub in the butter using your fingertips until it resembles fine breadcrumbs, then slowly add the milk to form a fairly firm dough.

2

Take the dough out of the bowl and knead it quickly on a lightly floured work surface, just enough to make it smoother. (When making any pastry crusts, it is very important not to over-work the dough as that will make the crust too tough.)

3

Wrap the dough in plastic wrap or a wax wrap and leave it to rest in the fridge for at least 3 hours before using it in your recipe. (Making the dough the day before would be even better.) Use the dough within 5 days. Shortcrust pastry freezes very well. Just defrost it in the fridge the day before you need it.

Biscuits

Whether sweet for dunking or savoury for eating with cheese, homemade biscuits are always a comforting sight and are quick to make. Here you will find one of each type. The classic shortbread biscuit is loved for its rich buttery flavour, and I also include an addictive savoury cracker to go with cheese.

SHORTBREAD

Enjoy this shortbread dunked in a mug of builder's tea – it's easy to make and you don't have to wait long to enjoy it.

MAKES 12 BISCUITS

150g plain flour, plus extra for dusting

a pinch of salt

50g caster sugar, plus extra for sprinkling

100g unsalted butter, cut into small pieces

You will need:

baking sheet

1

Preheat the oven to 180°C (160°C fan oven) Gas 4. Weigh the flour, salt and sugar separately, then sieve them together into a mixing bowl.

2

Rub in the butter using your fingertips until it resembles fine breadcrumbs. Gather the mixture together until it makes a stiff dough.

<u>3</u>

Put the shortbread onto a well-floured work surface and roll it out carefully until it is a rectangle, 1cm thick. Slide it onto a rectangle of baking paper, then mark it with a chopping knife to roughly outline the shape of the biscuits (rectangular strips) and prick it with a fork. Put the shortbread on its paper on a baking sheet. Bake for 15–20 minutes until golden brown.

<u>4</u>

Take the shortbread out of the oven and sprinkle it generously with sugar. Separate the rectangular biscuits using the chopping knife, then carefully transfer to a wire rack and leave to cool. Enjoy the buttery richness of your home-made shortbread!

WHEAT CRACKERS

I used to make these when I worked in the original St John's in Clerkenwell under the creative and inspired Fergus Henderson. Customers loved them so much that we never had enough and we were always trying to keep up with demand, making them every day by hand. You can make the cracker dough well in advance. It is unleavened, so it doesn't have to be baked straight away. The dough will keep in the fridge for 2 to 3 days. The crackers are excellent with cheese!

560g strong white flour, plus extra for dusting

1 tsp baking powder

8g natural fine sea salt

20g poppy seeds

20g cumin seeds

20g dill seeds

20g caraway seeds

1 tsp dried chilli flakes

80g/80ml extra virgin olive oil

You will need:

5cm pastry cutter

baking sheet

1

Weigh the flour, baking powder and salt separately, then sieve them together into a mixing bowl. Add the seeds and chilli flakes, then quickly mix the dried ingredients together.

2

Add the olive oil and 230g/230ml water. Using one hand in a circular movement, bring the ingredients together to form a dough.

3

Put the dough on a lightly floured work surface and knead it just enough to make it a bit smoother, for no more than 3 minutes.

4

Shape the dough into a ball, then wrap it in plastic wrap or a wax wrap and leave it in the fridge for 1 hour to relax.

5

Preheat the oven to 170°C (150°C fan oven) Gas 3 and line a baking sheet with baking paper. Take the dough out of the fridge and put it on a well-floured work surface. Roll it out to a thickness of approximately 5mm (you might have to divide the dough in half to make the rolling out easier).

6

Use a 5cm pastry cutter and cut out circles, rolling out and using the leftovers. With your rolling pin, roll out each biscuit as thinly as you can, then put the biscuits on the prepared baking sheet.

7

Bake the biscuits for 12 minutes or until they are a nice golden-brown colour all over. Transfer to a wire rack to cool. They will keep for a few weeks in a sealed jar or plastic container. This amount of dough will make loads of biscuits!

Sourdough Breads

I felt we should finish the book with a section on sourdough fermentation. This might be a bit of a challenge for people who have not baked sourdough breads before, but they are definitely worth a try. They are full of flavour, have a better consistency and are much easier to digest than the heavily yeasted commercial loaves to be found in supermarkets that can give some of us an unpleasant bloated feeling.

For thousands of years, sourdough was the only way to leaven bread. Ready-to-use yeast as we know it today is a relatively recent invention, dating back to the mid-nineteenth century, following the work of Louis Pasteur on fermentation, which explained scientifically what people already knew empirically. Before then, if you wanted a leavened bread, the dough had to be fermented with a wild yeast culture.

With the arrival of commercial yeast in bakeries, sourdough-making skills began to disappear rapidly, especially during the 20th century. But from the turn of the century onwards we've seen a big change in sourdough's fortunes, thanks to the passionate work of dedicated professional bakers, food writers and food historians to preserve that ancient technical knowledge. The general public's new-found eagerness to learn about all things sourdough ensures that the tradition of wild-yeast fermentation will continue through many fresh and keen adepts.

If you want to make sourdough bread, you will first have to get your own personal yeast going. This means that your first job will be to catch some of the wild yeast flora floating about in your kitchen then make them grow in number, and in that way in strength. This process takes seven days. It involves refreshing your starter (as it is called) daily with flour and water. You don't have to worry about using grapes, plums, apples or any other fruits, as there is more than enough wild yeast in your flour, the water, on your hands in your immediate environment to initiate fermentation.

SPELT STARTER

As a sourdough baker, you need to make your own ferment. This means that before you become a sourdough baker you will need to be a wild-yeasts farmer, whose main job is to harness a fraction of those microorganisms floating in the air and make them grow steadily in numbers to the point that they will be active enough to raise your breads. You can make a sourdough starter with any flour (even gluten-free), but I have opted for wholemeal spelt because of its nutty flavour. By using a wholemeal flour, you're also making sure that the wild yeasts living on the outside of the grain are now in your flour, thereby boosting your chances of initiating a natural fermentation.

MAKES 280G STARTER

140g spelt flour (used in 20g quantities)

20g fresh cloudy apple juice or a few drops of honey,
if needed

1

Put a small bowl on the scales and set it to 0g, then measure the flour. Set the scale back to 0g before measuring the next ingredient. Add 20g/20ml water to the bowl. (Adjust the temperature of the water according to your kitchen environment.) With your fingers, mix the ingredients together to combine them thoroughly.

2

Leave the mixture at room temperature with a lid placed slightly ajar over the bowl, or a damp kitchen cloth, to avoid your budding starter forming too much of a crust. Don't worry if that happens, however; just dissolve the starter in the next day's refreshment water. Basically, all you want at this stage is to encourage fermentation and to entice any wild yeast drifting around to join the party.

3

The next day, at about the same time, repeat process: add 20g/20ml water and 20g flour to your mixture from the previous day. By adding 40g of refreshment each day for six days, you should have 280g of an active starter by the end of the seventh day that will smell both sweet (the alcohol produced by the yeast) and sour (the acidity from the bacterial activity).

4

As the days go by, your starter should show signs of lively fermentation: it should be puffy, bubbly and its texture should be quite loose. If you feel that your starter is still a bit flat and sluggish three days after starting the process, instead of water, add the apple juice on one day, or a few drops of honey to the water to stimulate the fermentation by feeding sugar directly to your struggling yeast.

5

After refreshing your starter on the seventh day, leave it at room temperature for a few hours, then cover it tightly with plastic wrap or a lid and put it in your fridge to keep a healthy balance between the activity of the yeasts and the bacteria. That is exactly what sourdough is: wild yeasts and bacteria working together in symbiosis. The fermentation in your starter has been achieved, and you now have your 'mother' (culture). Your yeast is now ready to roll.

Caring for your mother culture

1

To keep your mother culture in tip-top condition, it is better to bake sourdough bread at least once a week, refreshing it ahead of your breadmaking session. With regard to how much flour and water should you use to refresh it before you bake, refresh it with the quantity you are going to take out to make a loaf on the day that you bake so that you don't end up with the culture growing exponentially.

2

If you're not able to bake on a weekly basis, this type of culture is flexible enough to stay idle for two to three weeks. If you're still not ready to bake at that point, you will need to refresh your mother to keep it 'motivated' and ensure that it doesn't lose faith in you! Alternatively, if you know you're not going to be able to bake for a while, you could freeze your mother. When you are finally ready to bake, just thaw it back to life and give it a feed to kick-start the fermentation again.

3

If your mother has been left ignored for a while, you might notice a sort of blackish water separating out on top of your starter. Don't panic! Your yeast culture is safe. This blackish water is called the 'hooch'; you just need to stir it back into the starter, give it a quick feed and your starter will be back in service.

4

As with any other dough, you can extend your fermentation for an even better sourdough taste. You could, after kneading, start the proving in a warm place for a couple of hours – enough to get the wild yeast going – and then place it, still covered, in the fridge to be kept for 8–18 hours at a controlled temperature to avoid any risk of over-proving.

5

When you are ready, take the dough out of the fridge for a couple of hours, to allow it to get to room temperature again, before proceeding with pre-shaping, bench-rest and shaping.

6

Alternatively, you could do things the other way around by fully proving the dough at the first rise and then shaping it but not completing the second rise as a shaped loaf. To do this, 1–1½ hours into the proving, put your bread in the fridge for 8–18 hours, then take your loaf out of the fridge for 2 hours before scoring it and baking it.

7

A third option is that you could have both the first *and* second rises take place in the fridge.

Now, it's time to make some sourdough!

WHITE SOURDOUGH

This is a good white all-rounder with a distinctive flavour and a dark crust. Please re-read the general information in the Basics chapter (on page 17) regarding kneading, proving, shaping and baking before starting the recipe to ensure that you are clear on all the technical points.

160g spelt starter (page 167), refreshed – see Tip page 177

470g strong white flour

30g rye, or any other wholemeal type of flour

10g natural fine sea salt

You will need:

proving basket or a mixing bowl lined with a tea towel

baking stone or an upturned baking tray

wooden peel, or baking sheet lined with baking paper

1

Put your mixing bowl on the scales and set it to 0g, then measure the starter. Set the scale back to 0g before measuring the next ingredient. Add 290g/290ml water to the bowl. (Adjust the temperature of the water according to your kitchen environment.)

2

Set the scale back to 0g, then add the flours. Put the bowl to one side and weigh the salt separately in a small bowl on the scales. (This makes it easier to correct in case you add too much on top of the other ingredients.) Add to the bowl with the flour.

3

Using only one hand in a circular movement, bring the ingredients together to form a dough. Put the dough on your work surface and, using the heel of your mixing hand, stretch it and fold it, or roll it back onto itself, then repeat the process, rotating the dough regularly to ensure that all the dough has been thoroughly kneaded. This should take 6–8 minutes; any longer than that would not benefit the gluten development or the volume of your loaf.

4

Scrape together all your dough to create a ball, then put it back into the bowl, cover it with a shower cap or plastic bag and leave it in a warm place to prove for 4–5 hours, folding it halfway through that first rise, until it has roughly doubled in size. Folding will help to improve the structure of your loaf.

5

Use a scraper to help you remove the dough from the bowl after that first rise onto a very lightly floured work surface. (As you become more familiar with baking, you might even skip that extra flour, because you'll gradually have learned not to automatically rely on its use.) Shape your dough into a round. Cover it again with plastic, then bench-rest for 10 minutes.

6

Use the palms of your hands to shape your loaf. With your palms flat and facing upwards, squeeze the left and right sides of the dough at the same time so that both sides are well stuck together. Now rotate the dough and squeeze again from the left and the right. Repeat this four or five times. Placing your hands on the sides of your loaf, give it three or four circular movements on the same spot, using the stickiness of the dough to tense the outside of the loaf. This completes the final shaping of your dough. This is your last opportunity to structure your loaf.

7

Once you have shaped your loaf, put it upside down, seam upwards, in a well-floured proving basket or a mixing bowl lined with a tea towel. Leave it for its second rise for 2–3 hours, depending on the ambient temperature until roughly doubled in size. If your kitchen is very warm, the loaf will prove much faster than if you were baking on a cooler day (see the temperature guide on page 32). Meanwhile, Preheat the oven to 240°C (220°C fan oven) Gas 9. Put the baking stone or upturned baking tray in the middle of the oven 1 hour before baking.

8

Now it is time to bake your loaf. Tilt your proving basket onto its side to gently tip the loaf onto the wooden peel, or prepared baking sheet. (If the loaf sticks to the basket, tickle it out very delicately with your fingertips.) (Alternatively, you can bake your loaf on a baking sheet if you don't want to use a baking stone or an upturned baking tray.)

9

With a corner of a razor blade held at a 45-degree angle, slash the top of the loaf with the pattern of your choice about to 2–3mm deep. These cuts are going to help the steam produced during baking escape in an orderly fashion without deforming your loaf.

10

Slide the loaf onto the baking stone or upturned baking tray. Spray the sides of the oven chamber to create steam. Bake the loaf for 25 minutes, then rotate the baking sheet or the loaf to help it to bake evenly and give it another 10–15 minutes, until dark brown and when you tap on the base it sounds hollow. It's up to you, but I would say that with sourdough breads, the darker the crust the better – a golden colour would make it a bit too chewy in my opinion. Cool on a wire rack.

TIP

The day before baking, refresh your mother culture using 80g flour and 80g water so that your fermentation is peaking again before measuring out the 160g you need for this recipe.

SPELT SOURDOUGH

This is a more wholemeal version of a sourdough bread. Spelt is a fabulous, primitive wheat, which is very nutty in flavour – the Romans' bread! You could replace the spelt with any other ancient grain, however, such as Khorasan (also known as kamut), einkorn or emmer, or simply use a wholemeal wheat flour, which will also work well.

You need to be aware that spelt is quite low in gluten, around 6 per cent whereas strong white flours start at about 12 per cent, peaking at about 18 per cent in Manitoba-type Canadian flour. It is also quite a fragile gluten, which means that it is better not to knead spelt doughs too much, or to leave them to prove for too long. The fragility of the gluten, however, makes it more digestible than white bread.

This recipe includes some strong white flour to make the bread a bit lighter in texture, and to remedy the lack of strength due to the low gluten in the spelt flour.

Please read the general information at the beginning of the book regarding kneading, proving, shaping and baking before starting the recipe, to refresh your memory on all the important technical points. Check the box on page 50 regarding water temperature.

160g spelt starter (page 167), refreshed – see Tip page 177

250g spelt flour

250g strong white flour

10g salt

You will need:

proving basket or a mixing bowl lined with a tea towel

baking stone or an upturned baking tray

wooden peel, or baking sheet lined with baking paper

1

Put your mixing bowl on the scales and set it to 0g, then measure the starter. Set the scale back to 0g before measuring the next ingredient. Add 330g/330ml water to the bowl. (Adjust the temperature of the water according to your kitchen environment.)

2

Set the scale back to 0g, then add the flours. Put the bowl to one side and weigh the salt separately in a small bowl on the scales. (This makes it easier to correct in case you add too much on top of the other ingredients.) Add to the bowl with the flour.

3

Using only one hand in a circular movement, bring the ingredients together to form a dough. Put the dough on your work surface and, using the heel of your mixing hand, stretch it and fold it, or roll it back onto itself, then repeat the process, rotating the dough regularly to ensure that all the dough has been thoroughly kneaded. This should take 6–8 minutes; any longer than that would not benefit the gluten development or the volume of your loaf.

4

Scrape together all your dough to create a ball, then put it back into the bowl, cover it with a shower cap or plastic bag and leave it in a warm place to prove for 4–5 hours, folding it halfway through that first rise, until it has roughly doubled in size. Folding will help to improve the structure of your loaf.

5

Use a scraper to help you remove the dough from the bowl after that first rise onto a very lightly floured work surface. (As you become more familiar with baking, you might even skip that extra flour, because you'll gradually have learned not to automatically rely on its use.) Shape your dough into a round. Cover it with plastic wrap or a bowl, then bench-rest for 10 minutes.

6

Use the palms of your hands to shape your loaf. With your palms flat and facing upwards, squeeze the left and right sides of the dough at the same time so that both sides are well stuck together. Then rotate your dough and squeeze it again from the left and right. Repeat this four or five times. Placing your hands on the sides of your loaf, give it about three circular movements on the same spot, using the stickiness of the dough to tense the outside of the loaf. This completes the final shaping of your dough. This is your last opportunity to structure your loaf.

7

Once you have shaped it, put it upside down, seam upwards, in a well-floured proving basket or a mixing bowl lined with a tea towel. Leave it for its second rise for 2–3 hours, depending on the ambient temperature until roughly doubled in size. If your kitchen is very warm, your loaf will prove much faster than if you were baking on a cooler day (see the temperature guide on page 32). Meanwhile, preheat the oven to 240°C (220°C fan oven) Gas 9. Put the baking stone or upturned baking tray in the middle of the oven 1 hour before baking.

8

Now it's time to bake your loaf! Tilt your proving basket onto its side and gently tip your loaf out onto the wooden peel or prepared baking sheet. (If the loaf sticks to the basket, tickle it out very delicately with your fingertips.)

9

With a corner of a razor blade held at a 45-degree angle, slash the top of the loaf with the pattern of your choice about to 2–3mm deep. These cuts will help the steam produced during baking to escape in an orderly fashion, without deforming your loaf.

10

Slide the loaf onto the baking stone or tray.

11

Spray the sides of the oven chamber to create steam. Bake the loaf for 25 minutes, then rotate the baking sheet or the loaf to help it to bake evenly and give it another 10–15 minutes, until dark brown and when you tap on the base it sounds hollow. In my opinion, with sourdough breads, the darker the better; a golden colour would make the bread a bit too chewy for my taste. Cool on a wire rack.

TIP

If you like, you can bake your loaf on a baking sheet if you don't want to use a baking stone or an upturned baking tray.

RYE PUMPERNICKEL

You definitely need a rye loaf in your baking repertoire. There are many rye bread recipes, especially when you research Eastern or Northern European baking. The reason for this is simple: rye is the only crop that will germinate when temperatures are freezing, so it was the only cereal that could be used for bread in colder areas. Wheat was originally grown only in southern Europe, having been first cultivated in the Middle East. As time went by, the wheat was hybridised to make it more tolerant of colder climes.

Rye, like spelt, is very poor in gluten, so there is no reason to knead it for long. When making pumpernickel, the kneading stops at simply combining the ingredients and spooning them into a well-oiled or paper-lined tin; in fact, the dough in this recipe is very much like a thick batter. The addition of sunflower seeds makes your loaf highly nutritious. Start preparations the day before.

160g spelt starter (page 167), refreshed – see Tip page 177

1 tsp honey

350g light rye flour

70g dark rye flour

100g sunflower seeds

9g salt

oil, for greasing

sunflower, sesame or poppy seeds, to sprinkle

You will need:

900g loaf tin

1

Take your starter out of the fridge and keep it at room temperature for 2–3 hours before using it in your bread.

2

Put your mixing bowl on the scales and set it to 0g, then measure the starter. Set the scale back to 0g before measuring the next ingredient. Add 450g/450ml water to the bowl. (Warmer water will speed up the proving.) Add the honey and stir well.

3

Set the scale back to 0g each time, then add the flours and sunflower seeds. Put the bowl to one side and weigh the salt separately in a small bowl on the scales. (This makes it easier to correct in case you add too much on top of the other ingredients.) Add to the bowl with the flour.

4

Oil a 900g loaf tin (if you have a non-stick tin you might risk not oiling it, but bear in mind that pumpernickel is very wet), or line it with baking paper. Pour or scoop your batter into the tin. Level it with a scraper dipped in water to prevent it sticking to the dough. Sprinkle the top with more seeds.

5

Cover with a shower cap or plastic bag and leave your loaf in a warm place to prove for 2–3 hours until it reaches the top of the tin or sticks out slightly over the top. Meanwhile, preheat the oven to 200°C (180°C fan oven) Gas 6.

6

Bake the loaf for 50–60 minutes. Spray the sides of the oven chamber to create steam three or four times at regular intervals throughout the bake, because rye breads love a hot oven, a long bake and a lot of moisture.

7

Leave the loaf in the tin on a wire rack to cool for 10 minutes, then turn out onto the wire rack to cool completely. It is better to leave a 100 per cent rye bread to settle for 10–12 hours before slicing it, because when freshly baked the crumb will be very sticky and the loaf can appear underbaked.

Postscript

Before you go …

I sincerely hope that you will enjoy making these recipes and that they'll give you, your friends, your family and perhaps even your work colleagues great satisfaction. As I've repeated many times throughout this book, these recipes are just foundations on which you can build your baking experience. Practise your breadmaking skills again and again until they become second nature to you. There will be some heroic failures along the way for sure, but keep persevering. There will come a time when the mistakes will be fewer and consistency in your baking will become the norm. And that moment is pure bliss!

I truly believe that the sight of a beautiful loaf, created with your own hands and mind, coming out of the oven with the fantastic smell of yeast and a caramelised crust is one of the most uplifting experiences in life. It is good for the body, and even better for the soul. So keep on baking!

Acknowledgements

I would like to warmly thank the people who have made publishing *Breaditation* possible. First of all, many thanks to Caroline Harrison, who accepted to collaborate with me on the project and has written a very thoughtful introduction for the book – and, yes, we will have those workshops happening eventually! Caroline wishes to acknowledge colleagues who researched and developed the treatments mentioned in the wellbeing chapter.

I also wish to express my most sincere gratitude for the work of Duncan Proudfoot and Zoe Carroll in supervising and enabling the publication of the book. Many thanks also to Jan Cutler for her thorough copy-editing.

I must mention the work of the whole team at Bread Ahead Bakery School and commend my colleagues for their total dedication in educating the general public and allowing a growing number of people to discover the joy of baking. Particular heartfelt thanks to baker extraordinaire Aidan Chapman who helped to set up the school from the very beginning and showed me the ropes of bread teaching.

Index

using the scraper 24, 25
knives, forks and spoons 54

lavash 97–100
liquid measurements 53
low mood, combating 12

mindfulness 14, 16
mixing bowls 53
mood elevation 11–12
mother culture *see* sourdough
    starter

negative thoughts 11, 12
no-knead baking 22

obsessive compulsive disorder
    (OCD) 13
occupational therapists (OTs) 9
olives
    ciabatta 63–6
    focaccia 67–71
oven
    producing steam 40–1
    proving in the 32
    temperature 45
overthinking 14

pastry brushes 55
pastry doughs 139–54
    puff pastry 141–7
    shortcrust pastry 153–4
    sugar pastry 149–51
peaceful place 11
pitta bread 93–6
poolish 101
post-traumatic stress disorder
    (PTSD) 8, 9, 10
preferment *see* poolish
proving 29–36, 44
    avoiding a crust 26, 31
    chilling the dough 30
    covering the dough 31
    fermentation process *see*

fermentation
    in the oven 32
    temperature 32, 44
    under- and over-proving 37
proving baskets 35, 36, 38, 54
puff pastry 141–7

razor blades 39, 45, 56
recipes
    bagels 81–5
    brioche 125–8
    bun dough 135–8
    ciabatta 63–6
    cinnamon scrolls 129–34
    English muffins 87–90
    focaccia 67–71
    Granary tin 111–16
    grissini 73–7
    lavash 97–100
    pitta bread 93–6
    puff pastry 141–7
    rye pumpernickel 185–7
    shortbread 157–9
    shortcrust pastry 163–4
    spelt sourdough 179–83
    sugar pastry 149–51
    wheat crackers 161–3
    white loaf 103–9
    white sourdough 173–7
    wholemeal loaf 117–22
rolling pins 55
rye flour 48
rye pumpernickel 185–7

salt 50–1
    effect on fermentation 50
    effect on gluten 51
    effect on yeast 50
    roles in baking 50–1
    sea salt 50
    table salt 50
scoring the bread 38–9, 45
scrapers 24, 25, 43, 54